The Tertiary College

Innovations in Education

Series Editor: Colin Fletcher (Senior Lecturer in the School of Policy Studies, Cranfield Institute of Technology)

There have been periods of major innovation in public education. What do the achievements amount to and what are the prospects for progress now? There are issues in each slice of the education sector. How have the issues come about?

Each author analyses their own sphere, argues from experience and communicates clearly. Here are books that speak both with and for the teaching profession; books that can be shared with all those involved in the future of education.

Three quotations have helped to shape the series:

> The whole process – false starts, frustrations, adaptions, the successive recasting of intentions, the detours and conflicts – needs to be comprehended. Only then can we understand what has been achieved and learn from experience.
>
> *Marris and Rein*

> In this time of considerable educational change and challenge the need for teachers to write has never been greater.
>
> *Hargreaves*

> A wise innovator should prepare packages of programmes and procedures which ... could be put into effect quickly in periods of recovery and reorganisation following a disaster.
>
> *Hirsh*

Current titles in the series

Garth Allen, John Bastiani, Ian Martin, Kelvyn Richards:
  Community Education
Bernard Barker: *Rescuing the Comprehensive Experience*
Julia Gilkes: *Developing Nursery Education*
Herbert Kohl: *36 Children*
Jan Stewart: *The Making of the Primary School*
David Terry: *The Tertiary College*
Paul Widlake: *Reducing Educational Disadvantage*

The Tertiary College

Assuring our future

David Terry

Open University Press
Milton Keynes · Philadelphia

Open University Press
Open University Educational Enterprises Limited
12 Cofferidge Close
Stony Stratford
Milton Keynes MK11 1BY, England

and
242 Cherry Street
Philadelphia, PA 19106, USA

First published 1987

British Library Cataloguing in Publication Data

Terry, David
  The tertiary college: assuring our future
  1. Education, Secondary — England
  2. Vocational education — England
  I. Title
  373.2′38′0942   LA635

  ISBN 0–335–10286–7
  ISBN 0–335–10285–9 Pbk

Typeset by Marlborough Design
Printed in Great Britain by St Edmundsbury Press, Bury St Edmunds

For Malley
without whom none of it would have happened

They formulated the doctrine that human institutions of language, custom and law are not of the magical character of taboos but man-made, not natural but conventional, insisting, at the same time, that we are responsible for them.

And there was, perhaps the greatest of all, Socrates, who taught the lesson that we must have faith in human reason, but at the same time beware of dogmatism; that we must keep away from both misology, the distrust of theory and of reason, and from the magical attitude of those who make an idol of wisdom; who taught, in other words, that the spirit of science is criticism.

Karl Popper, The Open Society and its Enemies.

Contents

Series editor's introduction

16–19 provision has always been much less of a contentious matter than 11–16 compulsory schooling. During the 1950s and early 1960s it meant sixth forms for the academically able. In the 1970s some 'open sixth' and 'one-year sixth' were added by schools which wished to. Meanwhile the symbolic significance of the sixth form had become huge. To have a 'good sixth form' meant that 'academic standards' were high lower down the school; that the school attracted gifted teachers whose special reward was to use their skills in near university-level teaching with small numbers: and that the much higher capitation for sixth-formers flowed into a funding otherwise wracked by hard times. Sixth forms were and are unquestionably a 'good thing' as far as schools are concerned.

Then along came 'falling rolls' like the 'wicked witch of the North', whose icy breath froze the sixth-form structure rigidly. Most schools accepted that there would be even smaller classes, and that some specialist subjects, like Spanish and drama, would only be available at nearby FE colleges or particularly well-equipped schools. Having 'tightened belts', as it were, more 16+ pupils wanted or needed a second chance at examinations, too. The numbers of school sixth forms did not shrink to vanishing point — they gently reduced or even remained the same as 'resits' stayed on.

The economic stringency of the era was often fended off by the taken-for-granted fact that sixth forms are a good thing. Local authorities faced fierce opposition to plans for merger or closure. New hostilities emerged with irate parents and governors equally determined to push 'value for money' as they were to uphold the traditional values so specially expressed in their sixth form.

David Terry is a perceptive and amused critic of the bluster in the recent past. He shows that small sixth forms are woefully 'inefficient' and that staff opposition to tertiary reorganisation is nowhere near as widespread as is propoganda to that effect. His main thrust, though, is that tertiary colleges are truly 'comprehensive' 16–19 educational institutes. Tertiary colleges, he says, combine the strengths of academic achievement and pastoral care of schools with the adult atmosphere and vocational practicality of FE colleges. He substantiates this claim from his experiences at Halesowen College. He provides practical guidance on how a college should be staffed and run, how big it should be and what aims there should be for staff–student relationships. A glance down the contents page shows that there is little, if anything, which he has avoided. To the best of my knowledge this is the first book on the tertiary college, and it wastes no time in getting straight to a discussion of the practical difficulties likely to be encountered in setting up such an institution. The author sticks his neck out in order to be clear about what really works.

Great attention is paid to students as adults and as union members, to personal tutors' responsibilities, to subject-teaching strengths and the tasks of the senior management team. Communications and the qualities of internal media feature particularly strongly. I believe that every member of staff in a tertiary college will find good sense and strong support in this book.

Tertiary alternatives, though, seem set to remain a local authority initiative and politicians will find the discussion of 16–19 initiatives most challenging. It takes courage to go beyond the 'cobbling together' of 'consortia' and the precious elitism of sixth-form colleges. Yet already in the late 1980s there are 50 or more tertiary colleges and by the year 2000 there could be more than 2,000 in England and Wales. If it were not for the capital costs of new buildings there would be hundreds already.

David Terry takes the reader through Halesowen College to show both the pitfalls and the possibilities – his whole argument is illuminated by Halesowen yet never dominated by it. Halesowen is not a test-bed for some future form. It is an innovation that has 'worked' and is working well as far as local politicians, staff and students are concerned. When I visited I sensed how normal and natural this achievement had become. I was struck again and again by the force of David Terry's main claim but expressed in a different way: why has 16–19 provision not been thought through comprehensively; what good arguments, if any, can be assembled *against* tertiary colleges?

Dr Colin Fletcher

Acknowledgements

My first acknowledgement is to Colin Fletcher, the editor of the series. I had not previously met him when he invited me, out of the blue, in February 1986 to contribute a book to the *Innovation in Education* series. I agreed without appreciating what I was letting myself in for — not having written a book before. Without his skilful blend of encouragement and criticism, I should not have succeeded.

I am indebted also to very many others. Most significantly to all who have helped to make Halesowen College such an outstanding success. The founding fathers are, of course, the Dudley Education Authority, its officers and members, who supported the initial concept and then, despite financial and political difficulties, stayed true to their promises and provided building and facilities that are the envy of most who visit us. At the risk of offending many who played a part in this, I would single out Ron Westerby, the chief education officer; Peter Metcalfe, the senior officer responsible at the time of reorganisation, who gave me marvellous personal support and did a magnificent job in securing resources for the college; Clive King, his assistant, who has been a constant friend of the college; Geoff Daniels, the present officer responsible for sixteen-plus provision. As is immediately evident to any visitor, the Dudley architects deserve great credit, and I would mention Peter Ellison and Alan Tyrls as well as their chief officer, Alan Powell. Officers in other departments have been equally helpful over the years, especially in finance and personnel, and our especial gratitude is due to Carol James and Tony Maher in finance.

A great advantage to the college has been the support it has had from local councillors regardless of party. It was planned under an

SDP chairman of education, Tom Clitheroe, strongly supported by the vice chair, Liz Walker (Conservative). Tom was also chairman of governors for the FE college, being succeeded by Albert Brodie (Conservative) in the year before the tertiary college opened. Albert continued as chairman during the first year of the new college. This was a crucial year, and he worked tirelessly, often being in college for over twelve hours in a day supervising the appointment of staff during a period of immense pressure. It was difficult to believe that he was in his seventies at the time! The indebtedness of the college to Albert is enormous, though probably appreciated to the full by only the small number who worked with him at the time. His successors have been no less stalwart in their support for the college. Peter Coleman (Conservative), Alan Hankon (Labour) and Alison Perks (Labour). Other governors too have been constantly supportive and I am glad to have the opportunity of expressing my appreciation of their work.

The all-party support has continued; the college has never been a political football, and it is a pleasure to be able to record the debt owed by the college to the present leader of the Dudley Council, Councillor Fred Hunt, Education Chair Councillor David Savage, and vice-chair and former mayor, Councillor Jack (JT) Wilson, and to their Conservative predecessors.

In the writing of this book I owe a great deal to a number of people, in addition to Colin Fletcher. To my wife, Malley, who was as closely involved in the book as she has been, and is, in other aspects of my work. She read all the drafts, and the final version is far better than it would have been without her constant advice and help. And without her encouragement, I should never have written it at all.

I am also much indebted to colleagues who read and commented on parts of the book, especially David Blades, George Kasper, Norman Cockin and Alan Hobday and to Barbara Hallam who proof-read the entire manuscript a few days before it was despatched, and in the light of whose comments dozens of infelicities were removed.

To Jane Rowell who prepared successive drafts of the typescript very special acknowledgement and gratitude is due. Invariably good humoured; she showed a near miraculous ability to decipher my appalling handwriting. Without her the book would certainly not have been delivered to the publishers on time, and I am deeply grateful and indebted to her.

The final acknowledgement must be to the students and staff of

Halesowen College, who have made it an unfailing joy to work in. To all of them, and to those listed earlier, I can say no more than a most sincere thank you.

Such mistakes as remain are mine. And I also accept sole responsibility for the opinions expressed freely in this book.

Introduction

It is almost as if the education system is attached to the rest of the country by a long piece of elastic: change in society generally is accelerating, but after initial inertia, the education system is being yanked in pursuit at an increasingly dizzy rate. To single out one of the many actual or possible changes and label it as more profound than the others might seem foolhardy. But institutional changes are profound — who would doubt the importance of introducing three types of school for the supposed three categories of child in 1944, or of replacing this system of grammar, technical and modern schools by single comprehensives in the 1960s?

From the mid-1960s, another institutional change, at sixteen-plus began and has been gathering speed ever since. And it may well turn out to be even more important than the move to comprehensives. In any event, it seems certain to continue. Many parents, pupils, teachers and councillors have already been involved in the turmoil of taking away sixth forms and concentrating sixteen-plus provision in separate colleges, and many more are likely to be. But the pace of change may be affected by government policies following the Conservative election victory in June 1987. Although continuing to press local authorities to economize, they are planning to give schools the right to opt out of local authority control. This new escape avenue for a school threatened with losing its sixth form could jeopardize any plan to rationalize sixth form provision, and already one authority, Nottinghamshire, has shelved plans to set up tertiary colleges.

Nevertheless, the secretary of state, Mr Kenneth Baker, claims not to be against tertiary and sixth-form colleges as such, and the pressures to concentrate sixteen-plus provision continue. And many authorities are currently planning to set up colleges, so their number seems certain to grow. And hence more and more people will find themselves caught up, in one way or another, in argument about sixth forms and their alternatives.

I make no claim to have written a comprehensive survey or to be objective and disinterested. Rather, I admit freely to believing deeply that the tertiary college, a comprehensive post-sixteen institution, has a unique potential to help the nation invest effectively in education and lay the foundations for a society that is compassionate, harmonious and united as well as creative, enterprising and diverse.

My justification for these claims rests on the experience of one tertiary college, at Halesowen near Birmingham in the West Midlands. While I have little direct knowledge of the thirty-five or so other tertiary colleges, I have every reason to believe that they, too, have achieved considerable success. But I also believe that Halesowen is unique in the extent to which it has developed a sense of partnership between students and staff.

Nevertheless, I believe that what I have written will be of interest to anyone involved in a sixteen-plus reorganization, whether as teacher or student, parent or local politician, as well as to anyone working in or associated with an existing college. While the examples given are all taken from practice at Halesowen, this is for purpose of illustration, not because I suppose our practice to be the last word on everything. Indeed, I am certain it is not the last word on *anything*, because every year we find ways of improving on virtually all that we did the previous year. One consequence of this book, I hope, will be the chance to benefit from criticism from a wider range of outsiders. Any readers who write to me about any aspect of Halesowen practice described in these pages will have their letters welcomed and read with care in the expectation of our gaining from ideas that might not have occurred to those of us working within the college. The middle is always a difficult position from which to observe the wood, and any view from the outside is likely to be illuminating!

There is another way in which the book is not a comprehensive survey, in fact not even of Halesowen College. The emphasis is on the full-time students in the sixteen-to-nineteen age range, not because other categories are unimportant but because one of my main concerns is to make a contribution to the argument about whether such students should be in school sixth forms or in colleges.

While I expect the book to be of interest to professional educators, I have tried also to make it readily accessible to readers with little or no knowledge of the English education system. Specialist terms have been explained when they first occur, often in a note. All notes are gathered together at the end of each chapter, and the index aims to be sufficiently comprehensive for the reader to track down the meaning of an unfamiliar term.

Given that so many of the examples are taken from Halesowen College, I had better say something about it, and the education authorities in England and Wales, identical with county or metropolitan councils, or boroughs as they are sometimes called (see note p. 13) for more on the system of local government). Dudley Metropolitan Borough is one such education authority. It was formed as a consequence of the reorganization of local government in 1974, largely from three ancient towns that had expanded to form a continuous urban area on the western edge of the West Midlands conurbation around Birmingham. These towns were Dudley, Stourbridge and Halesowen.

In the late 1970s, the new Dudley Education Authority removed the sixth forms from the schools in Stourbridge, setting up a sixth-form college alongside the existing college of further education. On turning their attention to Halesowen, the authority decided that as both the size of the Halesowen FE college and the number of sixth-formers were small, it would be better to put the two together and make a single sixteen-plus, or tertiary, college. A plan to do this was submitted for ministerial approval in 1980 with a proposed opening date of September 1981. The authority then took the unusual step of appointing a principal for the new college before ministerial approval had been obtained, and I started with the Dudley Authority in November 1980 as principal designate of the proposed tertiary college at Halesowen.

Four months later Secretary of State for Education and Science, Mark Carlisle, turned down the proposal, and I was left with a salary (for life!) but no job. It was then, with the approval and support of the Dudley Authority, that I embarked on the survey of teacher views on sixteen-plus reorganization that is referred to in Chapter 2.

The plan had proposed only that the sixth forms should be removed from the four seconday schools. As their age range was thirteen to eighteen, this would have left them as thirteen-to-sixteen schools, and it was this more than anything which led the secretary of state to reject it. However, he gave a clear hint that a reorganization proposal that also covered the schools would stand a good chance of succeeding.

Ron Westerby, only recently promoted to Chief Education Officer for the Dudley Authority, and not responsible for the incomplete and rejected plan, decided, the same day he received the letter of rejection, to try and get a complete reorganization proposal formulated in time to open the tertiary college in September 1982. The timescale was ridiculously short, and necessitated writing, in less than two weeks, a report on the whole of the Halesowen system, together with several options, each costed and with implications spelt out. Thanks to Ron himself and two officers, Harry Holt and Peter Metcalfe, this was done, and this second reorganization was indeed approved, by Mark Carlisle's successor, Sir Keith Joseph, but not until April 1982. Nevertheless, the new college opened only four months later in September 1982, and over the next three years the new school and college system for Halesowen gradually replaced the old.

This old system was itself the product of a reorganization of 1972 that was still incomplete ten years later. It consisted of four comprehensive schools for the thirteen-to-eighteen age range, one for girls, one for boys and two mixed. These schools were fed by middle schools for the nine-to-twelve age range, with primary schools below them.

Under the 1982 reorganization a system of four eleven-to-sixteen mixed comprehensives was introduced by a process which involved some mergers and some closures, with the middle schools disappearing altogether.

In 1981–2 there were less than 300 A-level students in the Halesowen schools and FE college combined, so an initial target for the new tertiary college was to attract at least that number on to A-level or equivalent courses. In our first year we fell short of the target number for first-year A-level students as most of those who were eligible tried to get into the established sixth-form college five miles away.

However, within two years we had achieved our target of 300 A-level or equivalent students, as well as maintaining the same number of vocational students as had been in the previous FE college. And in each year since numbers have risen sharply, already causing problems of accommodation and resourcing, despite the high standard of initial provision.

The popularity of Halesowen College is only incidental to the claims that Halesowen exemplifies how a tertiary should be set up and run. We have made mistakes and, we hope, learnt from them. I hope that this book will enable others also to learn, but from our mistakes not theirs.

Anyone likely to be involved in a sixteen-plus reorganization will first want to consider the arguments for and against school sixth-forms, and next whether a college should be sixth-form or tertiary. But then, assuming one is convinced that a tertiary college is the best option, will come the equally important questions about what aims the tertiary college should have, how it should be organized to achieve these aims, how the actual period of reorganization should be handled and, by no means least, how the college and the schools can work effectively together to provide the best possible education for all.

The format of the book follows this logical progression. While I could have said much more on nearly everything, I have tried to err on the side of brevity and to content myself with saying enough to illuminate but not to bore. But also, I hope, enough to convince the reader that the tertiary college does have a unique potential; and that the key to achieving this potential is to make relationships between members of the college, students and staff, a definite priority. Not that the tertiary college should aim at any sort of levelling in terms of attainment. Indeed, the exact opposite is the case. The aim must be to encourage excellence in every aspect of the curriculum and a constant striving by every student to achieve still more. But there is no contradiction in simultaneously insisting that every student, and indeed teacher, recognizes and respects talents, interests and abilities different from their own, and learns to work responsibly both as an individual and as a member of a team.

If I am right, such a college will provide not only a deeply valuable experience to the individual but also will make a vital contribution to the future of our nation, both by exploiting our human potential more effectively and by cementing relationships between people more securely. That is why I believe the tertiary college has a vital contribution to make to assuring a better future for our children and grandchildren.

David Terry
August 1987

PART ONE

Away with the sixth form

CHAPTER 1

The English education system and sixteen-plus provision

Change and the sixth form

SOS – Save Our Schools – proclaimed countless posters and stickers in the town we were passing through. Our American friends were bemused. Are wholesale school closures being planned? they wanted to know. No, none are to close, we told them, but they are to lose their sixth forms. Their what?

We explained that a sixth form is not in fact a form at all, but is simply a term used to denote all those who continue in a school after the legal leaving age of sixteen.

How many are in the sixth form of an average school? they asked. For a school of a thousand, probably about a hundred, we replied. It seems something of an overraction, they remarked, to talk as if a school is threatened with destruction when all that is planned is to remove 10 per cent of its pupils.

And so it is. Would there be as much opposition to removing a different 10 per cent, say the least academically able? Clearly not. So much for the comprehensive ideal of looking on all pupils as being of equal worth.

The term 'sixth form' is both archaic and misleading. Until the mid-1950s, the sixth form was a tiny elite preparing for university entrance, taking two-year courses leading to the Higher School Certificate or, from 1951, GCE A levels. In recent years schools have increasingly recruited one-year students, mainly to retake O levels or to progress to A levels from CSE.[1]

Before comprehensives, in the years immediately after the great

Education Act of 1944, all children were given a short intelligence test at the age of ten and the results used to direct them a few months later to one of two, or sometimes three, different types of school. The minority, and it varied anywhere between 15 and 40 per cent in different areas, went to grammar schools for a traditional education aimed at university entrance at the age of eighteen, or at any rate matriculation[2] at sixteen. These schools divided pupils into rigid streams, most having two, three or four such streams. The top stream largely went into the sixth form from the age of sixteen to eighteen; the lower streams left at the school leaving age – fourteen until 1948, then fifteen until 1972 when it was raised to sixteen.

In most places, the majority who 'failed' the eleven-plus (as the intelligence test became known) went to secondary schools for a curriculum largely based on the so-called three Rs – that curiously illiterate acronym for reading, writing and arithmetic. Secondary moderns did not have sixth forms.

Then came the move to comprehensives – common schools for all. Egalitarians and educationalists came to the same conclusion, but for different reasons. The former wanted equality in schools so as to lead to subsequent equality in society; the latter pointed out the practical impossibility of forecasting potential at the age of ten-and-a-half. The Crowther Report of 1959 compared schooling with scores in the Army and Air Force tests at eighteen – at a time of compulsory military service – and concluded that education and attainment correlate more closely with social background than with measured ability. Given that the eleven-plus was a simple test taken on a single day so that no account was taken of factors, such as health, that might affect the performance of ten-year-olds on that day, or of differing maturation rates, it is hardly surprising that the test turned out to be a pretty blunt instrument. As a consequence of Crowther, it became discredited as an instrument, and many no longer wanted such an instrument anyway.

So, in authority[3] after authority in the 1960s, separate grammar schools and secondary moderns were amalgamated to form comprehensives. Their ideal size was a matter of arithmetic: a three-form entry grammar school would have an eleven-to-sixteen population of 450 – assuming thirty to a form – and, if half stayed on for A levels, another ninety in the sixth form. If 25 per cent went to grammar schools, the new comprehensive would need a main school population of (4 × 450) 1,800 to produce a sixth form of ninety.

But few authorities had existing buildings capable of housing a school of this size; and those that built, or proposed building, new schools for this number of pupils found a general fear that they would be too large and pupils swallowed up in an impersonal anonymity. In fact, those schools of 2,000 or more pupils that were set up proved rather successful. But few were, and most of the new comprehensives had between 1,000 and 1,500 and, consequently, only about thirty to forty A level pupils in each year of the sixth form.

Bolstering the sixth

Despite the considerable enthusiasm in the 1960s for comprehensives as common schools where children of all classes, aptitudes and abilities would learn and develop together, no one seems to have remarked that their sixth forms were not in the least comprehensive, containing only that minority – usually less than a quarter – who had the motivation and academic ability to aim for A levels. The majority either left education altogether at sixteen, or continued as full- or part-time students at technical colleges – later renamed colleges of further education (FE).

Subsequently, however, schools did try to enlarge their sixth forms, especially following the raising of the school leaving age to sixteen in 1972, by adding to their range of courses and encouraging students to take only one or two A levels together with lower level courses, or to stay on for one year only. Most of these new sixth-formers, as they were called at the time, took one-year O-level courses, either to improve grades obtained at the end of the fifth year or to convert CSE to O levels. And usually with a staggering lack of success. Nationally published figures are a clear indictment of these one-year courses, with pass rates often around 30 per cent.

Not that the schools readily admitted their failure with one-year sixth-formers. Headteachers in their reports at speech days often omitted any reference to their examination results, while dwelling on those of two-year A-level students. Furthermore, the proudly proclaimed pass rates at A level had much more to do with the school's entry policy than with anything else: the more rigorously border line candidates are excluded, the higher the pass rate tends to be.

Boosting pass rates by not entering borderline candidates is one way in which the interests of the individual can be subordinated to those of the institution. This happened even more blatantly in the careers advice given to pupils at fourteen or fifteen, the main object of which appeared to be to ensure that all those with the remotest chance of taking a sixth form course should do so – unless, of course, they were considered trouble-makers. Few schools allowed the local further education college to be advertised on an equal footing with their own sixth form, and to this day there are schools that do not permit staff from the local college to set foot in the school.

This indefensible practice declined in the 1980s, not because of public outcry at the scandal of it, but because sharply falling numbers caused by a decline in the birth rate coincided with a period of financial stringency and led to the realization that even quite large sixth forms were inefficient. In the 1960s and 1970s many young people had their interests sacrificed to the need to maintain sixth-form numbers, while in the 1980s their counterparts were saved by the need to economize. In neither case did the interests of the young concerned appear to be the first consideration.

Consequences of size

Even without financial pressure or falling rolls, the arithmetic of sixth-form provision is compelling. Not many would think that a sixth form should offer fewer than sixteen A-level subjects – indeed most would feel that more than this number is desirable.[4] Using school time-divisions, eight forty-minute periods a week is a normal allocation for an A level subject. Local authorities usually allocate teachers on a ratio; and one teacher for every twelve sixth-formers is fairly common. If we assume the average number of A-level subjects taken by students is 2.5, that is half take three and half two, that for an average of five periods a week students are in groups of twelve for tutorial work, games, general studies, additional O levels and other support studies, and that each teacher teaches thirty-two periods a week, teaching-staff requirements for different sizes of sixth form can be compared and shortfalls or surpluses deduced (Table 1).

The break-even point, on these assumptions, is with about sixty A-level students in *each* year. So a sixth form with fewer than 120 students who are each taking a minimum of two A levels is demonstrably inefficient.

Table 1   Sixth-form numbers and staffing

A-level students per year	Teacher-periods needed per week			No of periods available on 1:12	Shortfall (−) or surplus (+)	
	to run 16 subjects	for other work no of groups (12 max) x5	Total		Periods	Teachers
20	128	10	138	53	−85	−2.7
40	128	20	148	107	−41	−1.3
60	128	25	153	160	+7	+0.2
80	128	35	163	213	+50	+1.6
100	128	45	173	267	+94	+2.9

Incidentally, it needs to pe pointed out that while the shortfalls shown in Table 1 are genuine, the surpluses are not entirely so. With more than sixty A-level students it is likely that there will be more choosing the most popular subjects than can reasonably be taught in one class, and all or nearly all the surpluses shown will be needed for running two or more classes in these subjects. This, of course, allows a given subject to be placed in more than one group (often called a block) of subjects, or two or more ability sets can be run in the same block. With the very much larger numbers in a sixth-form or tertiary college, *both* of these can be done for many subjects – as well as adding to the number of subjects – thereby increasing the number of different combinations of subjects that are possible as well as making grouping for teaching more efficient.

Another way of showing the disadvantage of small sixth forms is to look at average class size (Table 2). The same assumptions hold as for Table 1. If there are n students averaging 2.5 A levels each for 8 periods a week for each A level this implies $20n$ ($2.5n \times 8$) student-periods a week. But 16 A levels implies a *minimum* of (16 × 8) 128 class-periods; thus the *maximum* mean class size is $20n/128 = 5n/32$. As before, the figures for 80 and 100 students would be reduced as a consequence of running more than one class in some subjects. But the figures for 20 and 40 students are dramatic and indisputable.

Table 2   Sixth form numbers and class size

No of A-level students per year (n)	Mean class size for A levels
20	3
40	6
60	9
80	12.5
100	16

Both Tables 1 and 2 show the dire effect of a reduction in numbers. And the efforts of headteachers to increase numbers by widening the range of courses is of no avail: efficiency comes from larger numbers on the same course; having more courses merely replicates the inefficiencies across a greater number of different types of course and student.

Despite the recruiting and propaganda to which schools subjected their fourth and fifth-year pupils, sixth forms in many areas shrank; not only because of falling rolls but also because more and more young people chose to transfer for A levels and other courses to the local FE college. Schools were driven to expedients and, incredibly, to claiming these expedients were educationally sound. The number of periods taught for each student was often reduced; the ability range within the class increased – there would, for example, no longer be a separate group for further mathematics, so it had to be taught in the same class as single-subject mathematics; and in some subjects first- and second-year groups were combined. At the same time, general studies was usually cut back so that the total number of taught classes for each student was reduced.

The replacement of the system of separate grammar and secondary modern schools by area comprehensives often had the incidental effect of increasing the number of small sixth forms. In the 1960s it seldom happened that the number of comprehensives was the same as the number of grammar schools in the previous system; usually some of the secondary moderns also became comprehensives, acquiring sixth forms in the process, thereby ensuring an increase in the number of schools with sixth forms and therefore a reduction in their average size, or at any rate in the average number of A-level students in each.

The search for alternatives

By the 1970s the prospect of falling numbers was beginning to alarm the planners, and some of the later comprehensive reorganizations did seek to concentrate sixth-formers so as to maintain viable sixth forms. Secondary moderns became eleven-to-sixteen comprehensives feeding into the sixth form of an eleven-to-eighteen comprehensive. Some went further and replaced a system with two single single-sex grammar schools by one of a single eleven-to-eighteen comprehensive fed by several eleven-to-sixteen comprehensives. This concentrated sixth-form provision but at the cost of a disparity of esteem between the schools. Invariably the comprehensive with the sixth form was more highly regarded than the others, and this was resented by the latter. Lacking a sixth form itself, a school no longer had any vested interest in recruiting its fifth-form leavers, so schools that lost their sixth forms on going comprehensive were often prepared to let the local FE college advertise itself to their fifth-formers, and large numbers promptly chose to go there. The attraction was not the range of courses at the college so much as the fact that it was a college not a school. Few wanted to leave one school only to enter another.

A fairer system, both for the schools and their pupils was to concentrate all the sixth-formers not in one of the schools but in a separate college – a sixth-form college. This system became increasingly popular in the late 1960s and by the mid-1970s there were over 100 sixth-form colleges in England and Wales usually with more than 200 A-level students in each year and therefore able to offer incomparably better provision than even the largest school sixth form. Over twenty-five A levels in virtually any combination was the norm, as well as a general studies programme of great richness. A-level pass rates and university entrances were impressive. The success of sixth-form colleges with A-level students cannot be doubted.[5]

Often a sixth-form college would be set up at the same time as the grammar and secondary moderns were replaced by comprehensives. If the college was located in one of the schools, almost invariably the former boys' grammar school was chosen. The old boys' association would often be the most powerful local lobby against change and it could, to some extent, be placated by concentrating all sixth-formers there. Many sixth-form colleges today bear the names of former boys' grammar schools.

In law, sixth-form colleges are schools in that the set of legal requirements applicable to them is the same as those for all other schools – the School Regulations. The other set of regulations, Further Education Regulations, governs polytechnics and colleges of further education. Local educational bureaucracies were usually rigidly divided into schools and further education branches – indeed many still were in the mid-1980s, as was the Department of Education and Science.[6] This division made officialdom excessively slow to consider the needs of sixteen- to eighteen-year-olds as a whole.

To those who did it was apparent that there was a considerable overlap between school or college sixth forms, on the one hand, and colleges of further education on the other. Often the FE college would have the largest number of sixteen to eighteen year-olds taking A levels, not merely the largest number of the age group in education. If sixth forms were to be removed from schools there would be obvious advantages in having a single post-sixteen college rather than a sixth-form college and FE college side by side.

The first authority to set up systems including a single post-sixteen college was Devon, at Exeter in 1970, followed by Barnstaple in 1972 and Bridgwater in 1973. Neighbouring Somerset followed with similar colleges at Strode in 1973 and Yeovil in 1974; and Lancashire with Nelson and Colne College in 1972 and Accrington and Rossendale in 1975. The heads of these colleges determined that, although legally FE colleges, they must have a new and distinct image. And a special name. Tertiary[7] was chosen, as signifying that they followed on from primary and secondary as the third stage of comprehensive education. This choice was not entirely a happy one as tertiary was already in use, especially in Scotland, to denote post-eighteen education at university, polytechnic and elsewhere. But the idea was wholly laudable; and the term has stuck.

During the 1970s sixth-form college reorganizations were mooted in many areas and several leading educationalists advocated their advantages and forecast the demise of the school sixth form, at any rate in the state sector. The political parties at that time, however, avoided expressing an opinion.

The consortium case

Heads of schools with sixth forms felt threatened and, in many places, banded together to plan rearguard action. Often the nature of this action implicitly conceded the main plank of the reformers' case, namely that sixth forms were too small. Neighbouring schools explored the possibility of running their sixth forms in common; as a 'consortium' was the term. Thereby, it was claimed, each school could continue to enjoy the benefits of having a stake in a sixth form, with sixth-formers on the premises, while planning would be for the larger number obtained by pooling the sixth formers of several schools, thus ensuring a wide range of courses and their economic provision. Many such consortium arrangements were set up in different parts of the country, and a good number were still in existence in the mid-1980s.

A sixth-form consortium is, essentially, a split-site sixth-form college, but usually having as many heads as there are participating schools. A split-site is difficult enough, and can only enlarge the range of provision for students if the timetable allows time for movement between sites. Some authorities recognized this and appointed a separate head of the sixth-form consortium. However, the heads of the participating schools usually retained, probably inevitably, much of their autonomy and this impeded unified planning.

In a consortium each head is expected by his or her staff to bargain with the other heads so as to obtain only advantages from the arrangement. To gain another subject at A level is acceptable; to lose one the school is already running is not. So if each school is already offering A level French, each will probably continue to do so in the consortium; but if only one is offering A level Italian, this is an addition to the range offered by the consortium and also an improvement to efficiency if Italian numbers increase as students from the other schools take it.

If. Usually the increase is zero – and for several reasons. First, there is no incentive for staff to advise students to take subjects in another school in the consortium. Second, even if it is possible to fit Italian in, the student may well be deterred by having to commute and by the thought of going some of the time to a strange school where the surroundings, the students, the staff and the rules are all unfamiliar. Third, the student may well find that the timetable does not allow the subject to be taken with the other subjects chosen. This will probably depend on whether there is a separate timetable for the consortium.

There are four tests of any consortium arrangement. The sincerity of the schools can be gauged by whether advice to fifth-formers is comprehensive and unbiased, covering equally the local FE college, training schemes and subjects available at other schools in the consortium. The commitment of the participating schools can be tested by whether there is a single separate timetable for the consortium with all the schools having common times of day. The effectiveness of the consortium can be tested by two further questions. How many A level subjects have been terminated in some of the schools to allow concentration in the others? And, lastly, how many students actually do take subjects at more than one school? On one recent visit to a school participating in a sixth-form consortium, my request to travel on the interschool minibus, to see how many students were using it, caused embarrassment. None did.

Most consortia would fail all these tests. The only one I have come across that did not was in the city of Cambridge where the local education authority had the good sense to set it up in a way that was designed to prevent individual heads cheating and with an independent secretary whose job was mainly to see fair play. Yet even that one was felt, in the mid-1980s, to be ending its useful life and the authority was planning to reorganize its colleges and schools so as to make it unnecessary.

Rural exceptions

A sixth-form consortium is likely to be little more than cosmetic. In view of this and the incontrovertible arithmetic of small sixth forms, can there be any case at all for retaining sixth forms in schools? Yes. In a small rural town distant from other towns and supporting one eleven-to-eighteen comprehensive, there may be no reasonable alternative. In such a circumstance, it is clearly the duty of the authority to provide sufficient staff at the school to enable sixth-form provision comparable with what can be achieved much more economically in urban areas by setting up a college. And they must ensure that there is ready access to vocational courses, either by bussing to the nearest FE college or by providing them in the school itself. Particularly in rural areas, self-study programmes using local radio could well enhance the range of courses. The success of the Open University, and the new Open College,[8] should encourage the development of such courses, and there is a wealth of experience in other countries that needs to be studied and adapted.

But at sixteen students are prepared to travel, and the college option is therefore available in most areas. Then the pros and cons of school sixth forms and of different types of college can be discussed in earnest. The attachment of schools to their sixth forms, and the opportunities afforded by the obligatory consultation procedures for local opinion to be voiced, virtually guarantee heated debate whenever a sixth-form reorganization is proposed. Whether this leads to either consensus or rational decision-making is another matter, and it is to the conduct of the public debate preceding any sixth-form reorganization and to a consideration of the arguments advanced that we turn in the next chapter.

Notes

1. Until 1951, pupils of university potential took the School Certificate examination at fifteen or sixteen and Higher School Certificate two years later. Five subjects had to be passed to obtain a School Certificate, and two for a Higher Certificate. These were replaced by the General Certificate of Education (GCE) at Ordinary (O) level and Advanced (A) level, but there was no stipulation on the number of subjects to be passed. However, the minimum for university entrance was five at O level and two at A level (or equivalent). O level was aimed at the top 20 per cent of the ability range. The Certificate of Secondary Education (CSE) was introduced in 1965 for the next 60 per cent of the ability range in each subject, with a correspondence between CSE and GCE being agreed, so that a grade one at CSE was equivalent to a grade C or above at O level. In 1986 the GCE O level and CSE were merged to form the General Certificate of Secondary Education (GCSE), which had an increased emphasis on course work (Examinations are also discussed in Chapter 11, p. 177).

2. Originally the minimum entrance qualification for Oxford or Cambridge, obtained either by special examinations set by the universities or, more usually, by obtaining the School Certificate or, later, obtaining grade C or above in five GCE O level subjects or grade one at CSE. Later 2 A level passes were required as well.

3. County or Metropolitan District Councils with responsibility for, among many other things, education are called Local education authorities when dealing with education. In 1987 there were 104 education authorities in England and Wales.

4. See Chapter 5 for a further discussion of curriculum issues.

5. See Chapter 2 p. 17 for a 1986 ministerial view. But in *Crisis in the Sixth Form* (1981) – see Bibliography – Fred Naylor seeks to demonstrate that sixth-form colleges get poorer results than grammar sixth forms.

6. The 1985 edition of *Education Statistics for the United Kingdom* did not once mention either sixth-form or tertiary colleges, despite the fact that by 1985 tertiary colleges had existed for fifteen years and sixth-form colleges for over twenty.

7. This designation seems to have been first suggested by the distinguished educationalist, Sir William, later Lord, Alexander, in 1969 when he proposed a new set of regulations for the sixteen-to-nineteen age range. His eminently sensible suggestions have still not resulted in any government action and provisionfor the age range continues to be governed by either Schools or FE Regulations.

8. The Open College is a government scheme being launched in September 1987 under which colleges and private agencies can provide courses dovetailed into national TV and radio programmes.

CHAPTER 2

Decapitating schools

I worry not about the setting-up of colleges but about decapitating schools.
Sir Keith Joseph, Secretary of State for Education and Science, 1984.

Reorganization: procedure and practice

Almost perversely, the procedures laid down by the 1944 Education Act positively encourage opponents of a school reorganization to impede change. Both local and national government must approve, not only a closure, but also any significant alteration in age range or nature of intake, and there have to be periods of public consultation lasting two or three months. The procedure is complicated, cumbersome and slow. As a consequence, reorganization often begins amidst a storm of protest and is completed too late.

First, the local education authority must approve one or more schemes of reorganization as options. These must then be the subject of widespread local consultation for a minimum period of three months, after which the authority determines which one, if any, it wishes to proceed with. The proposal is then sent to the secretary of state for education and science, and a further minimum period of two months is allowed for objectors to express their views direct to him (or her).

The national school inspectorate, Her Majesty's Inspectors of Schools (HMI), scrutinize the authority's proposals and report in confidence to the minister, and it is highly likely that there will also be representations through the minister's political party. The minister can suggest modifications to, as well as approving or rejecting, a reorganization proposal. From the first vote by the local authority to ministerial approval can easily take two or three years.

Opposition to removing school sixth forms and concentrating post-sixteen work in one or more colleges will come from several quarters. Teachers, parents, governors, former pupils and present pupils are all likely to be represented in the forces seeking to resist change. Often one of the political parties will ally itself with the opposition. And the local press may well be unhelpful by encouraging forms of protest that can be photographed and arguments that can be fitted into a headline.

Chief education officers have become more adept over the years at navigating these turbulent waters. It is essential to avoid the whole show being hijacked by a furious minority. The first attempt to reorganize at Halesowen, in 1980–1, failed when the then secretary of state, Mark Carlisle, rejected the proposal. Second time around, the authority set out an impressive timetable of meetings: there were three at every one of the nearly thirty schools affected, one for teachers, one for parents and one for governors. Having been hounded by a travelling clique the first time, it was decided that each individual should be entitled to attend one meeting only. And this was enforced. I was present at a meeting for parents when one vociferous member of the audience was required, by the chairman of the education committee, who was chairing the meeting, to leave on the grounds that he had been present at an earlier meeting for teachers. He was both a parent and a teacher, and could attend either meeting, but not both. The enforcement of this rule had the effect of showing that opposition was much less widespread than had been supposed.

Distaste at the methods used by some defenders of school sixth forms must not lead to their arguments being brushed aside. In order both to gain as much acceptance as possible and to set up a new system that is as good as possible, it is important to appraise rationally the arguments advanced against reorganization.

The inefficiency of small sixth forms was discussed in the previous chapter. Before reorganization at Halesowen, the chief adviser for the authority showed that the unit costs in the smallest sixth form were over five times those at the authority's sixth-form college, *and* the range of the curriculum was very much smaller. Nor can anyone creditably defend giving biased careers advice to fifth-formers. Other matters, however, are less clear-cut.

Continuity and examinations

Some will argue that the students themselves will suffer; that transferring at sixteen to a college will introduce discontinuity in curriculum provision and in pastoral care. In the school, it will be said, there will often be the same teachers in the sixth form, and in any event the curriculum will have been planned as a continuum from O to A level; and pastoral care in the school, depending on a continuity of knowledge built up over the years, will be much better than in a college where the staff have to start afresh and have insufficient time to get to know students. Although the amount of continuity in even the best of schools is probably exaggerated, there is force in this argument, and the college must do what it can to set up effective liaison with the schools to lessen discontinuity and to avoid becoming a short-stay transfer institution where students are never really known by staff. Against this argument it can be pointed out that there may be gains in making a fresh start, provided essential information is transferred; and many students positively like moving to a college at sixteen.

Certainly examination statistics do not give any support for the claims that the break at sixteen is educationally harmful. With examination results it is notoriously difficult to be sure one is comparing like with like. Nevertheless, the A-level results for the Dudley Authority for 1986 are worth quoting. The authority is made up of three historically distinct towns, Dudley, Stourbridge and Halesowen. In 1986, the first had schools with sixth forms, the second an established sixth-form college and the last a growing four-year-old tertiary college. The percentage pass rates at A level in that year for students on two-year courses who started with at least five O levels were respectively 62 for the school sixth forms, 87 for the sixth-form college and 79 for the tertiary college. The difference in the figures for the sixth-form and the tertiary college is probably entirely the result of differences in policy between the two colleges. The tertiary college admits to an A-level course anyone with a reasonable prospect of success, whereas the sixth-form college unashamedly seeks to cream off the most academically able so that, while 5 O levels is their general minimum entrance requirement, in fact 6 O levels or grade B are commonly demanded. So the tertiary college has a larger proportion of weaker students – most of whom nevertheless succeed – and furthermore makes no attempt to boost pass rates by excluding borderline candidates from being entered.

There is little national evidence available on examination successes, the Department of Education and Science (DES) being singularly unhelpful in not publishing data separately for schools, sixth-form colleges and tertiary colleges. However, the text of a speech given in October 1986 by Mrs Angela Rumbold MP, the second-ranking minister at the DES, included the following: 'There appears to be no statistically significant difference between the [A-level] performances of tertiary colleges and sixth-form colleges or between tertiary colleges and comprehensive schools.'

Leadership training

Examination results are not, of course, the be-all and end-all of education. It will be argued that the sixth form provides a peculiarly valuable training in leadership and responsibility that cannot be replicated in a college. The good school can indeed, by virtue of the relatively small number of sixth-formers and the presence of younger pupils, give the seventeen- and eighteen-year-olds a sense of seniority within a community that can bring out the best in them. It has, I think, to be conceded that there cannot be opportunity in the college to provide exactly this sort of experience, although it is certainly possible to do a great deal, especially in a tertiary college, to give students experience of responsibility and service. A major theme of this book is the importance of this and ways in which it can be done.

Against this it can be said that not all schools do all they could to give such an experience to their sixth-formers; and by no means all sixth-formers want to have this sort of responsibility anyway. Moreover, fifth-formers can be given similar responsibilities. And this may be better; for they include all the age group whereas the sixth form is a minority only, and nowadays fifteen-year-olds may be more prepared to undertake, and more likely to gain from, prefectorial responsibilities. Certainly the heads of many eleven-to-sixteen schools feel so.

The presence of near-adult students of seventeen or eighteen in a school does, of course, exercise influence over younger pupils. Defenders of school sixth forms argue that this is invariably benign, adding to the academic atmosphere, setting standards in the academic, cultural and sporting areas of the school, encouraging pupils to stay on for higher education. On the other hand, it is a matter of observation that many schools seem to hide their sixth-formers away from the main school, presumably so that younger pupils will not be inclined to emulate less desirable aspects of their elders' behaviour. The sixth-former as someone younger pupils can look up to is more myth than reality, and there does not seem to be any evidence that discipline is better in schools with sixth forms or that the staying-on rate is higher. Indeed, the staying-on rate seems invariably to increase when a break at sixteen is introduced.

Teachers and teaching

It is argued that teachers teach better to those below the age of sixteen as a result of having some sixth-form teaching. A-level teaching, it is said, is stimulating, and teachers who do it are therefore more stimulating when teaching younger pupils. Three observations are pertinent. First, it is difficult to believe that someone with a degree in a subject could find A-level work as other than relatively elementary. The intellectual stimulation of teaching should come more from devising ways of making concepts accessible at elementary level, and whether the level is A or O is irrelevant to this. Second, the sixth form is such a small proportion of most schools that only a minority of teachers in an all-through school can have the benefit of the alleged stimulation of sixth-form teaching. Third, teaching to a variety of different ages and levels is by no means necessarily to the advantage of the learners. I well remember a student who had recently transferred to Halesowen College, having started her A-level course in a school sixth form, telling me that she felt that in her school the teachers were constantly finding difficulty in adjusting their teaching to the frequent changes in level; that her sixth-form teachers usually arrived having just taken a main school class, and it showed. Of course, it may well be that what teachers mean is that sixth-form teaching is an oasis of calm in the demanding and exhausting round of main-school teaching. I have a good deal of sympathy with this; but if that is what is meant, let it be said.

Perhaps unsurprisingly, it is clear that teachers find colleges attractive and congenial places to work. Is there not, therefore, a danger that the schools will suffer in a reorganization by losing all their best staff? Not as great as might appear. Concentrating sixth-formers brings considerable economies of scale and far fewer teacher-hours are needed overall than were in the previous school system: if four French classes of three or four each are replaced by one set, the need for French teachers for these students is only a quarter of what it was.

College principals nodding agreement at my assertion that O-

and A-level work are equally elementary to the graduate specialist teacher might care to reflect on one consequence. When recruiting for college posts, lack of post-sixteen experience should be no bar to appointment. Recognition of this would remove one objection teachers can have to sixteen-plus colleges, namely that teachers get trapped on one side or the other of the break at sixteen and their career opportunities are curtailed.

I suspect that what underlies the opposition of teachers to losing contact with the sixth form largely stems from the greater prestige – and salary – that the British attach to teaching older pupils. This has implications for the relationships between teachers in the schools and the college: it is of the greatest importance to strive for a relationship of equality and to avoid any suggestion that the college is somehow innately superior to schools for the lower age-ranges. This association of institutional standing with age range is one reason why schools fight fiercely to keep their sixth forms. It therefore behoves all who are advocating a reorganization to sixteen-plus colleges to demonstrate by both word and deed their belief in the equal, if not greater, importance that should be attached to the teaching of younger pupils. It is surely indefensible to value the pinnacles of the system more than the foundations on which they rest. This, no doubt, derives from the dominance that the universities, especially the two ancient ones, have exercised over our education system.

Research project

The English seem to prefer not to resolve arguments on education by discovering the facts. Admittedly there are considerable difficulties in collecting objective data on examination results or staying-on rates, and a study producing valid results would be expensive. Easier to study are the views of teachers before and after reorganization. In 1981, together with Derry Watkins and Helen Weinreich-Haste of Bath University and funded by the Dudley Authority, I carried out research on teacher views in several different areas, and during the following two years a good deal of data was amassed. The next part of this chapter gives the results that are particularly relevant here.

The first and main part of the research was conducted in four areas without school sixth forms, two having a system of schools feeding a sixth-form college, two a system with a tertiary college.

As a control, a similar inquiry was carried out in four areas with all-through schools.

In each of the areas with a break at sixteen, a personal approach was made to the principal of the college. All four generously agreed to help, and this help was crucial to the research. First, their advice was sought as to which schools would form a representative sample of the main feeder schools, and they were good enough to effect an introduction to each of the heads of these schools. The heads were then visited to ask for their personal assistance and all generously agreed.

It was explained to the heads and principals that our aim was to sample the opinion of about 15 per cent of their staff, and that we wanted a sample that was biased towards senior staff. Our specification was that the sample should contain all the deputies, two heads of major departments, the teacher in charge of careers, with the rest chosen to include some experienced and some inexperienced teachers. Quite deliberately, then, our sample of staff opinion in each school and college contained a disproportionate number of senior staff. We introduced this slant for a number of reasons. We wanted to explore perceptions about a wide variety of possible effects of reorganization and senior staff are likely to have thought more about these than their junior colleagues. Also, senior staff will probably have taken the lead in consultations at the time of reorganization and have continued to lead opinion since. However, sufficient questionnaires were returned by junior staff for us to be able to see whether there were any significant differences between the views of junior and senior staff.

We thought it important to include all the deputies. If the school had two deputies, one labelled pastoral and one academic, their views might differ significantly on some matters. Similarly, we specified that the two major heads of department should come from oppostie sides of the science/arts divide.

The heads and principals nominated the staff who would best fit the sample criteria for their school, and nearly all those nominated agreed to take part. Before the questionnaires were issued, the staff concerned were given a general information letter and one of us was available to meet them, either as a group or individually. Many fears were allayed by this procedure, and a response rate of over 95 per cent was achieved.

The heads and principals, however, were not asked to complete questionnaires. Instead, we asked them to take part in a taped interview during which discussion ranged over all the questions in the questionnaire in a relaxed and conversational way.

The towns

The four areas chosen for the main research were all places where sixth forms had been removed from the schools with the setting up of separate colleges, but were otherwise as different from each other as possible. They were all in different education authorities, none of them Dudley.

Area A was an established industrial area forming part of a large industrial conurbation. Much of the housing was of poor quality and the environment was generally drab and depressing; a typical Labour heartland. The purpose-built sixth-form college occupied one of the best sites in the area and was a well-designed building of the late 1960s, which had happily escaped the earlier fashion for great expanses of concrete and glass. In competition with colleges of further education, it was fed by over twenty secondary schools, each mixed and having a twelve-to-sixteen age range. Some of these schools were formerly grammar schools, but most were secondary modern and had, therefore, never had a sixth form. The reorganization was substantially completed in 1972. The college had about 1,150 students, all full-time. Eight schools and the sixth-form college took part in the research.

Area B was a pleasant small town, with a population of about 30,000, set in rolling countryside and some distance from any large centre of population. Agriculture and related industries were important local employers, but many commuted to work in industry and commerce elsewhere. The tertiary college was purpose-built as part of a leisure and arts complex central to the cultural and recreational life of the town. Facilities in the college were excellent. It had five main feeder schools, two of which had previously been selective. All had become mixed eleven-to-sixteen comprehensives. The college had 950 full-time students and around 2,000 part-time. The reorganization had been completed in 1975. Three schools and the college took part in the research.

Area C was an old industrial town with a population of about 110,000 and at some distance from other urban areas. A large, purpose-built tertiary college was opened in the early 1970s to serve the needs of most of the sixteen- to nineteen-year-olds. While this college was the sole provider for much of the town, there was an

FE college and a school sixth form in competition with it. Because of geography, this competition was greater in some areas than others. Some of the twenty or more principal feeder schools were formerly selective, but most were secondary modern. The age range for all of them had become eleven to sixteen and they were mixed. The college had about 2,000 full-time and 10,000 part-time students. The reorganization was completed in 1974. Six schools and the college took part in the research.

Area D had a population of about 85,000. Tourism was the main industry, and the town was also a substantial dormitory area for a major industrial conurbation some twenty miles away. Before the reorganization there were two single-sex grammar schools and mixed secondary moderns. One of the grammar schools became the, mixed, sixth-form college; the other became a single-sex comprehensive. This school was included in the research, together with the other three comprehensives, all mixed and 11–16, and the college. The college had just over 500 students. The reorganization had not been completed until 1982, so the college still had a fifth form, the remnant of the former grammar school, at the time of our research.

As a control, we surveyed staff opinions in six comprehensive schools with sixth forms in four different parts of the country. These four places were chosen to be as similar as possible to the four areas, A to D, described above. The heads of the schools chosen were approached and asked to help in the same way as the heads of the other schools had been. Two refused, but the rest agreed readily, and they and their staff were most cooperative, so that we obtained a similar response rate, of over 95 per cent, to our questionnaires.

College systems overall

We expected to find that staff in the all-through comprehensives would see little or no merit in removing sixth forms from schools and concentrating sixteen-plus provision in separate sixth-form or tertiary colleges, and it is to this aspect of our survey that I turn first.

The final question on the questionnaire given to staff in the all-through schools asked them to imagine a system based on a break at sixteen being set up in their area, with their school losing its sixth form, and then to estimate how good this system would be compared with the present one. The responses from their staff to this admittedly very general and hypothetical question are given in Table 3 below. Remarkably, less than half of these teachers felt that 'decapitating' their own schools would necessarily be a bad thing – and 16 per cent actually thought it would be an improvement! This suggests that there is a silent majority of teachers in all–through schools who are not as totally opposed to proposals to remove the sixth forms from their schools as in commonly supposed.

Table 3   Staff in all–through schools: expectation of reorganization based on a break at sixteen (percentage of respondents)

Much worse	5
Worse	43
Neither better nor worse	36
Better	16
Much better	0

How did those actually working in colleges or eleven–to–sixteen schools respond to the same question? This is shown in Table 4 below, where the Table 3 figures are repeated for ease of comparison. (In questionnaires to staff in reorganized areas, we used 'successful' rather than 'better', etc. In the tables they are assumed to mean the same thing.) If it had been reasonable to expect a strongly negative view of 'decapitating' schools from staff in schools with sixth forms, it seemed even more reasonable to expect such a view from those left in eleven–to–sixteen schools. In fact Table 4 shows the opposite, with only one in five of our sample considering their own system to be unsuccessful or very unsuccessful.

Table 4   Perceptions of break-at-sixteen system (percentage of respondents)

	All-through schools	11/12–16 schools	Sixth-form or tertiary college
Very unsuccessful	5	1	0
Unsuccessful	43	20	7
Neither good nor bad	36	39	7
Successful	16	35	54
Very successful	0	5	32

Admittedly, some of these eleven-to-sixteen schools had not lost sixth forms, having been secondary moderns all along. And even in those that had, some staff had arrived after the reorganization. We analysed the responses from these different categories, and did indeed find a more pessimistic assessment from staff who had been left behind in a school after it lost its sixth form, but the differences were not large, and the overall impression remains of there being much greater satisfaction with school/college systems than is usually assumed – even from those in the eleven-to-sixteen schools.

Since sixth-form teaching is often looked on as a perk, it is less surprising, perhaps, that few of those working in the colleges looked on the system as unsuccessful; but the size of the favourable majority is notable, with no fewer than 86 per cent considering it as successful or very successful.

On the basis of replies to this single question, then, it does appear that the fears of staff in all-through schools about systems involving separate sixth-form or tertiary colleges are not generally held to be realized by those working in such systems. But enthusiasm is greatest amongst those working in the colleges.

Who gains?

We did not define 'better' or 'successful' in this last question, but earlier questions had been more specific, and respondents had been asked to judge the effects of a break at sixteen on four separate categories. Table 5 shows the results, collapsed to a three-point scale. As we already know from Tables 3 and 4, the expectations of teachers in all-through schools are more pessimistic than the perceptions of staff in reorganized areas. But the difference varies,

Table 5   Overall effects on pupils, students and staff (percentage of respondents)

| | | Expectations of staff in all-through schools | Perceptions of staff in reorganized areas | |
			School staff	College staff
For pupils in the sixteen-minus schools	Harmful	79	36	14
	Neutral	17	37	40
	Beneficial	4	27	46
For students in the colleges	Harmful	41	19	2
	Neutral	30	21	11
	Beneficial	29	60	87
For staff in the sixteen-minus schools	Harmful	92	45	36
	Neutral	8	39	46
	Beneficial	0	16	18
For staff in the colleges	Harmful	24	18	11
	Neutral	32	20	13
	Beneficial	44	62	76

as these tables show; and there is a measure of agreement between the staff in the different systems.

Less than half of any of the categories of staff think that pupils in the sixteen-minus schools actually benefit, the gloomiest and the rosiest views being taken, respectively, by staff in all-through schools and staff in colleges, none of whom actually work in such a school! Of those who do work in the sixteen-minus schools, 36 per cent feel the lack of a sixth form to be harmful, 27 per cent think it is beneficial and 37 per cent are neutral. Perhaps this is the range of verdicts most deserving of respect; and it is one that confirms neither the pessimism of the all-through staff nor the optimism of the college staff.

On the effects on students in the college there is also some agreement. Only 41 per cent of the all-through staff thought they would be harmed, 60 per cent of sixteen-minus staff felt they had benefited, and no less than 87 per cent of the staff actually in these colleges agree.

Not surprisingly, the staff in all-through schools are very pessimistic about the effects on those who end up teaching in the sixteen-minus schools, with 92 per cent expecting them to be harmed. While the staff in reorganized systems are less pessimistic, the figures are hardly cause for satisfaction, with small majorities in both schools and colleges feeling these staff have not gained and may actually have lost out. When we come to the last category, the effects on staff in the colleges, there is a general agreement that they will not lose, and may gain, by working in a college.

Ingredients of success

Returning to the general question at the end of our questionnaire, it is relevant to this book to separate the results from each of the four

Table 6   Overall views on reorganization expressed by school and college staff in areas with colleges (percentage of respondents)

	A	B	C	D
Unsuccessful	11	8	25	9
Neither good nor bad	26	15	26	23
Successful	63	77	49	68

Giving a clear order of popularity
1. B   System with small tertiary college
2. D   System with small sixth-form college
3. A   System with large sixth-form college
4. C   System with very large tertiary college

areas with a break at sixteen. Again reducing to a three-point scale, we obtained the figures in Table 6.

So it would appear that size, rather than whether the college is a sixth-form or tertiary, is the important factor. This interpretation is confirmed by Tables 7 and 8. Table 7 contrasts the different types of establishment. The differences between the responses are not great; but analysis by size of college (Table 8) tells a different story.

Table 7 Overall view of reorganization: sixth form versus tertiary (percentage of respondents)

| | Areas with | |
	sixth-form colleges	tertiary colleges
Not successful	10	17
Neutral	25	20
Successful	65	63

Table 8 Overall views of reorganization: large versus small colleges

| | Areas with | |
	large colleges	small colleges
Not successful	17	9
Neutral	28	20
Successful	55	71

The interviews with the headteachers largely confirmed the staff views, with the important difference that heads in eleven-to-sixteen schools were generally more pleased with the new system than were their staff. Not surprisingly, most support for the new systems came from heads of schools that had not lost a sixth form in the process of reorganization. Previously these schools had been made to feel inferior to schools with sixth forms; now all the schools were equal. But most of the headteachers of schools which had lost sixth forms did concede that there were gains, and some admitted that having a sixth form was something they had enjoyed but which might be of doubtful benefit to the young people themselves. Many observed that no system would be best for every pupil, but that one based on a break at sixteen was the most suitable.

Several of the heads of schools feeding a tertiary college commented that a single institution post-sixteen had the advantage of preventing a student from making the wrong choice between a sixth form or sixth-form college on the one hand and an FE college on the other. One told of a student going to the FE college because her friend had gone there rather than the sixth form which was eminently more suitable for her. A number of heads of schools that formerly had sixth forms admitted that advice to pupils on what to do after sixteen was now much better as it was no longer necessary to try to persuade them to stay on in the school's sixth form.

Nearly all heads agreed that discipline had not deteriorated when the sixth form was taken away, but also observed that there had been benefits for the sixth-formers in being leaders of the school. Yet they also agreed that it had been difficult, if not impossible, to have a school ethos appropriate to the needs of both thirteen- and eighteen-year-olds. And they all agreed that the absence of a sixth form enabled the school to give responsibility to fifth-formers, and encouraged them to act responsibly. Some, however, felt the academic atmosphere of a school was poorer without a sixth form, with teachers aiming to achieve no more than the minimum necessary for the pupils to gain admission to their desired course at the college, whereas had they been going into the school's sixth form the teachers would have striven to give them a flying start.

Nevertheless, the overall impression of interviews with all the headteachers was of the new system being imperfect but a definite improvement. The variation in response between the different areas was similar to that of the staff responses discussed earlier, with a preference for small colleges rather than large ones, but with some agreement on a tertiary college being preferable to a sixth-form college.

The first half of this chapter described and commented on the objections likely to be raised to any proposal to concentrate post-sixteen provision in a college or colleges. The second half reported research which shows, in the sample surveyed, that staff opinion generally is nothing like so hostile as it might seem. More importantly, it showed a strong preference, from those who ought to know, for smaller colleges, and also suggested that liaison between schools and colleges leaves a good deal to be desired, with the large college doing worst. There would seem to be lessons in this both for the nature of reorganization proposals and for their implementation. The research is, however, generally neutral on one crucial question, namely whether sixth-form or tertiary colleges are to be preferred. So what are the pros and cons?

The only general argument in favour of a sixth-form college is that it can provide a studious atmosphere uniquely valuable to academically able young people taking A levels and aiming, in the most part, to continue into higher education; and that in the tertiary college the presence of less academic students makes this sort of environment impossible. Yet, as has been shown, there is no evidence of any significant difference between the A-level results of comparable students in the two types of college. As far as I know, no sixth-form college principal has ever maintained that there is any such difference. Other things being equal there is, therefore, no argument from examination results for a sixth-form college. This is not, of course, to denigrate the work of existing sixth-form colleges but rather to maintain that there is no good general reason for founding new ones.

What are the arguments for a tertiary college? First, the wider range of courses enables a student to take a mix of so-called academic and vocational courses and, in particular, to bridge the gap between the theoretical and the applicable. Second, having in one institution young people with a wide range of abilities and aptitudes makes it possible to encourage a sense of working together for a common purpose among not just a favoured minority but everyone. Who can doubt that these two divides, between the academic and the vocational and between managers and workers, have greatly disadvantaged our country and go a long way to accounting for our national decline in the last forty years?

Of course, simply putting all post-sixteen provision in one institution and labelling it a tertiary college does not guarantee, of itself, that anything will be done to bridge these two divides. It merely presents an opportunity that cannot be present in a sixth-form college. Much of this book is about how a tertiary college can be organized to serve these vitally important ends while at the same time encouraging the flourishing of excellence in individual attainment and providing a uniquely valuable preparation for adulthood and citizenship.

PART TWO

Tertiary reorganization

CHAPTER 3

Shaping the beginning

Sixth-form colleges separate out the academically more able at sixteen; tertiary colleges keep the sixteen- to nineteen-year-olds together. It is therefore paradoxical that the major development in sixth-form colleges should have been in the 1960s when comprehensive schools were in fashion because they promoted equality, whereas tertiary colleges increased in popularity during the next two decades at the same time as excellence replaced equality as the educational vogue word.

A sixth-form college is easy to define: it is simply a school for sixth-formers. Not that all are identical. Some seem to aim for academic excellence to the virtual exclusion of all else and seek to admit only students taking two-year A-level courses, often with stringent entry qualifications such as six O levels. Others have tried to broaden out and include many one-year students not taking A levels and, possibly, possessing no O levels at all. But none would take more than half the age range, and most less than a quarter, so even with open access, they cannot be said to be comprehensive institutions. And what is almost entirely missing from all sixth-form colleges is a range of full and part-time vocational courses.

Nevertheless, all but a handful of sixth-form colleges describe themselves[1] as being 'open access'. But since their range of courses cannot possibly meet the needs of anything like all the sixteen-year-olds in their areas, this phrase must represent more of an aspiration – and presumably a tertiary aspiration at that – than a reality. And only one college, the tertiary college at Leigh, in Lancashire, states that 'Students are placed in [the] most appropriate course. If none [is] available they are advised which other college to go to.' There are two sixth-form colleges in Wigan, and they *both* claim to be open access![2]

What is it?

The simplest definition of a tertiary college is that it is a comprehensive post-sixteen institution, providing full- and part-time
academic and vocational courses to meet the needs in a locality of
all, or nearly all, people aged over sixteen and with no upper age
limit. In order to run vocational courses and to accept part-time
students it needs to be run under further education regulations.
Thus a tertiary college is a further education college, but not,
despite the Department of Education and Science, vice versa. The
early pioneers of tertiary colleges laid great emphasis on the tertiary
college as a very special sort of college under further education
regulations. They formed an association, known first as the
Tertiary Colleges Panel and later as the Tertiary Colleges
Association (TCA). They clearly saw it as fundamental to their
concept of a tertiary college that it should not be in significant
competition with any other institution, whether school or college,
mainly because they wanted to see an end to the separation of
academic and vocational students at sixteen and to the biased advice
often given to fourth- and fifth-formers as a consequence.

The first constitution of the Association stated:

> For the purposes of this Constitution, a Tertiary College is
> defined as an establishment within the maintained sector of
> education and normally under Further Education Regulations
> which is the sole provider in its catchment area of post-16
> education, other than that which may be found in separate
> establishments of higher or adult education.

But it was soon recognized that few tertiary colleges could meet
this criterion, and the following clause was added:

> Some colleges which do not necessarily meet the criterion of
> 'sole provider', but are nevertheless associated with an 11–16 or
> 12–16 comprehensive system and are predominantly concerned
> with post-16 education other than higher education, may be
> deemed to be Tertiary Colleges for the purpose of membership
> of the Association.

And this was followed by the rider: 'The Committee of the
Association shall have the sole right to decide whether a college
should be admitted to the Association under this provision', which
has the merit of completing the circularity.

Some tertiary college principals felt this definition, although logically impregnable, to be somewhat lacking in information content. We, therefore, proposed the following:

A tertiary college shall be defined as a single institution in the maintained sector of education that is: under Further Education Regulations; providing all or nearly all the full- and part-time education sixteen-plus for the given locality; organized so as to maximize the availability of different combinations of courses and subjects; dedicated to breaking down barriers and promoting equality of opportunity between students of different aptitudes, abilities, skills, ages, sex, race, religion and social background; developing courses that seek to meet flexibly the needs of everyone over the age of sixteen in its locality; developing courses that span the divide between the theoretical and academic on the one hand and the applicable and vocational on the other.

Although the TCA, for reasons which escape the author, rejected this proposal, and decided to stay with their comfortable tautology, it is a definition with which few tertiary college principals would disagree. I do not doubt that it is this concept of a tertiary college that made tertiary colleges rather than sixth-form colleges increasingly attractive in the 1980s. First the Liberal Party espoused them – modesty forbids an explanation – then its Alliance partner, the Social Democratic Party, and then the Labour Party. And while the Conservative Party had no national policy, many tertiary colleges, including the one at Halesowen, came into being under a Conservative council – and it was a Conservative secretary of state who approved over forty tertiary reorganizations in the early 1980s.[3]

Despite its general acceptability, a tertiary college defined as above could take many forms. Or, perhaps, it is precisely because the definition does not narrowly prescribe a form that it is acceptable. Be that as it may, a tertiary college could be the sole sixteen-plus institution in a small town remote from others and have 500 or 600 full-time students aged under nineteen, half of whom would be recognizable as possible sixth-formers, as well as perhaps three times that number of part-time students, some daytime but most adults coming for evening classes. This, to some, is the model for a tertiary college. But many are very different, perhaps by being much larger or having a bigger proportion of part-time students, by providing a whole host of activities such as playgroups, meetings and activities for minority groups, and care for elderly or handicapped people. In urban areas, one tertiary college may be part of a group of colleges which together provide a comprehensive range of educational and community services for a population of a quarter of a million or more. And many have to use more than one site: Leigh has eleven; and Oswestry one main site with two nearby annexes and a third twenty-three miles away!

Some colleges also have significant numbers of full- and part-time students aged over eighteen and taking courses up to, or even beyond, degree level. Blackburn College, for example, describes itself as 'an institution of tertiary and higher education'. The question of whether the essential nature of a tertiary college is compatible with its also being a higher education college may become academic, as the secretary of state is currently proposing to separate out higher education from further education – advanced further education (AFE) from non-AFE (NAFE) as they are unprettily termed in the trade. My own view is that this separation is desirable in general but should not be applied rigidly. A small proportion of post-A-level courses will do no harm, but the bulk of the full-time students need to be in the sixteen-to-nineteen age range in order to be able to realize the sort of college that this book seeks to describe.

My own direct experience of working in a tertiary college is confined to only one, of medium size, largely on one site, and not forming part of a group of tertiary colleges. I shall, therefore, mainly write about setting up and running a college like this. But first I want to make some points about planning and implementing a reorganization that are applicable whether it is a sixth-form or a tertiary college that replaces the school sixth forms.

At the risk of seeming perverse, I would assert that the first objective must be the schools. They are going to lose the argument, their sixth forms, and some of their best teachers. There is an obvious danger that the prophecies of dire consequences for them will turn out to be all too accurate. A second objective is to set up the college. This depends on getting the premises, equipment and staffing right, and on doing everything possible to get the future staff and students looking forward positively to working in the new college. Thirdly, and most importantly, there must be transition arrangements to ensure that those caught up in the reorganization do not suffer.

Planning: the principal

There are a number of essentials. Starting with the new college; it really must be new. Not, in fact or appearance, the old FE college writ large. If the new college is to be a tertiary, it must not be headed by the principal of the college of further education on which it is based. However talented he (and it will almost certainly be a 'he') may be, fears of an FE takeover will have been confirmed by his appointment. If he wants to be a tertiary college principal, let it be elsewhere. This objection does not apply to a school head; indeed the appointment of a school head may well be reassuring to those who want the tertiary college to be as much like a school as possible.

But there is another objection to appointing *anyone* local. It is that all the local heads and principals will almost certainly have been involved in the debate preceding reorganization, and will be seen by many as being tainted with partisanship, or even, however unfairly, as being actuated by self-interest. It is much better to appoint a complete outsider, who can come with clean hands and with no local suspicion of his or her motives.

In the management structure of a new tertiary college it is equally essential to demonstrate that there has not been a takeover by the former FE college. The old college must be formally closed and a new college, with completely new structure of management and of organization of teaching sections, must be founded. It is not only to avoid the image of 'FE takeover' that this is essential: if the old college is not destroyed both in name and structures, it will continue to have a *de facto* existence, and will inhibit new developments. However, this objection does not apply to allowing a sixth-form college to grow out of a school by ceasing to admit new pupils under the age of sixteen, because a sixth-form college is simply a school consisting entirely of a sixth form.

But, except in law, a tertiary college is not simply an FE college with a particular range of ages and courses. In the case of a tertiary college replacing an FE college, there is no compelling reason why the new college should prefer as a precedent practices in the former college rather than those in one of the school sixth forms. It has replaced both types of provision, and must appear even-handed between them. And when staff in the soon-to-disappear college ask whether they will have to apply for their old jobs, the reply should be that they cannot, as their jobs will disappear with the college. Like their colleagues who will be coming from the schools, they can only be promised jobs comparable to those they have already. To do more would be to place them in a privileged position compared with their colleagues from the schools. And that would be both morally wrong and a recipe for factionalism in the new college.

It is particuarly tempting not to set up a new system when a reorganization involves a large and successful FE college which already has a substantial number of A level students. It will be felt, with reason, that the successful management system of the college should not be destroyed out-of-hand; and it will be argued that, since most of the staff in the new college will come from the existing one, there will be great advantages in allowing them to continue in a system they understand and have confidence in.

Yet the bigger and more successful the existing college, the greater the fears of an FE takeover will be, and the more important it is to abolish the old college and found a new one in its stead.

If this is too bold for the LEA – which, being ultimately a committee, may not be very good at grasping nettles[4] – the best alternative is to leave the existing college as it is and set up another college alongside. This new college could at first be no more than a sixth-form college under Further Education Regulations, but if it is firmly tied into the existing college it should be able to develop a wide enough curriculum range – with some subjects taken at its larger neighbour – to justify its being called a tertiary college.

Should such a satellite college have its own principal? If it does, the usual failure of heads of institutions to cooperate more than merely superficially will impede its development. If it does not, and the head of the existing college is also principal of the new one, everyone will cry 'FE takeover'. My own view is that the principal of the existing college should be legally head of the new one as well, but that for all intents and purposes it should have its own head, designated as principal of the new college but actually an extra vice principal of the existing one. This principal/vice principal should be paid an additional amount to make the salary up to principal level. If the two colleges are given a common governing body, it should divide itself into two large sub-committees to act as separate governing bodies for the two colleges. This should enable the new college to avoid being seen as a mere appendage of the existing one while reducing the risk of a wasteful duplication of courses. More importantly, it should enable objective and important advice to be given to students as to which college is the better for them.

Management systems are discussed in more detail in Chapter 10; here it is appropriate to consider the question of staff appointments. Senior ones are, of course, crucial; none more so than the principal of the tertiary college. That this should be an external appointment has already been argued. Because a tertiary college runs under further education regulations, it is sometimes assumed that previous experience of FE is essential. This is a mistake. The regulations are not particularly difficult to master, and if the new college is to be perceived as merging the best of FE and school traditions, the top post must be open equally to applicants from either sector. Indeed, there are some very definite advantages in having a school background, as the author did when starting at Halesowen. This will be reassuring to those who feared that the best of school traditions would be ignored, and a school person will have a flying start in liaison with schools.

However, provided the person appointed is not from the old college, ability is more important than background. It cannot be said that education authorities have been spectacularly successful in appointing heads of schools and colleges. More than one report in the 1980s pointed out the unsatisfactory state of appointment procedures. The appointing panel is usually comprised of local politicians, with education officers attending in an advisory capacity. It is unlikely that anyone present, apart possibly from the candidates, will have been a college principal or indeed the head of any school or college. Few education officers have been heads or principals; indeed most have not even been deputies. Sometimes the panel will not even have taken the trouble to have a preliminary meeting to agree what qualities they are looking for and what criteria are to be used to judge whether the candidates possess these qualities.

Quite often the education authority is almost dilatory in its work. Some still use a standard form for *all* teaching appointments and give no indication of what they would like covered in any accompanying letter of application. I know of none that take the trouble to visit the candidates in their present schools or colleges, where far more could be learnt in half a day than from any form or reference. Nor does it ever seem to occur to the authorities to seek outside help. A college principal will have responsibility for an annual budget of anywhere between 2 and 10 million pounds and for an organization with hundreds of staff and thousands of students. It seems little short of criminal to penny-pinch on appointing. Yet it would not be difficult to seek help from experienced officers and advisers in other authorities or from successful principals, retired or active, for relatively modest sums in expenses and consultancy fees. For a few thousand pounds an authority could get a small team, mainly made up of outside experts, to produce a short-list based on appraisals of the applicants in their present posts and to brief and advise the appointing panel. Successful companies would not dream of treating such an important appointment in the casual and amateurish way that is still all too often the norm in education.

Nor, of course, would they dream of giving tenure for life virtually regardless of subsequent performance. All heads and principals ought to be on renewable contracts, and paid more because of this. There are, admittedly, both difficulties and dangers in putting school heads and college principals on fixed-term renewable contracts. An efficient and fair system of appraisal would be needed, and setting up such a system would pose considerable problems. What are the criteria by which a head or principal should be judged? I doubt whether a general consensus could be found on this; and if it were, it might well be a compromise that would exclude the more colourful and charismatic. And there would be considerable danger in leaving the decision solely in the hands of the education authorities, committees of local councillors.

A few years ago I visited a large junior college in California. The principal impressed me as a person of great drive, imagination and personality, and I was also impressed with the college. He was on a renewable contract. The first period had been for five years, the next for two, and when I met him he was halfway through a period of only one year. He did not expect his contract to be renewed, and was actively engaged in looking for another job. From what he and others told me, no one seriously questioned his professional competence. The school board had turned against him for political reasons – he had been too outspoken in his reservations about some of their policies. The board was expected to appoint as his successor someone more circumspect and malleable.

The way in which one or two local councils in England in the mid-1980s treated their headteachers lends credence to the view that, in their present form, they cannot all be trusted to undertake responsibility for fixed-term contracts for their senior staff. The only satisfactory answer is for the system of local government to be reformed, including the introduction of proportional representation so that the council is less likely to be hijacked by an extremist minority, for there to be a much greater interest from the general public in the local council, and for more people of calibre to be prepared to put themselves forward for election. In the meantime, a system of short-term, say five-year, renewable contracts for heads and principals needs to be introduced, but it could not be left entirely in the hands of the local authority. The secretary of state and the national inspectorate – the HMI – would need to be involved.

A final thought on this subject is that if it is ridiculous to let an incompetent head or principal continue in office, it is equally ridiculous to compel a competent one to retire merely because a rigidly prescribed retirement age has been reached.

To return to the question of staff appointments on reorganization, there is one lamentable tendency that needs to be resisted. It is to give senior positions to people for no better reason than that they have been left stranded by the reorganization. During the 1960s, many new comprehensive schools were saddled with former heads given the courtesy title of 'associate head' and an undefined role. Almost invariably disastrous they were too, distorting the management system as the new head devised ways of bypassing the 'associate' he or she had been saddled with. Not infrequently they were a focus of discontent and a considerable obstacle to development. For the same reasons, a blend of compassion and cowardice, this sort of thing still happens. No one should have any job, let alone a senior one, for any reason other than merit. Stranded heads and deputies should either be pensioned off, or taken into the advisory service as extra to establishment where they might well be able to do valuable work and retain their dignity. The extra expense is peanuts compared with the total cost of the reorganized schools and college, not to mention the large numbers of young people whose futures depend on the new system working well from the outset.

So an authority should have a policy of outside appointments to the principalships of its new tertiary colleges. And not merely have such a policy, but proclaim it. One incidental gain will be to give added authority to those FE college principals who argue for a tertiary reorganization. Precisely because it is known that they will not become principals in the system they advocate, their arguments will be imbued with the authority of the truly disinterested.

Staffing principles

It is, however, reasonable to reserve jobs not for individuals but for categories. It is highly desirable to have rough parity in the new college between local school and college appointments to the senior positions. And it should be openly specified that, for example, of the two vice principals, one should be from the local schools and one from the previous FE college and of the, say, five third-tier posts, at least two should be from each sector. The unions may not like this, but it is far better to be open about it than to encourage suspicion and recrimination subsequently.

Only the college necessarily has new posts – and all of these need to be treated as such. The schools will be in this position only if there is some reorganization of their sector in addition to the sixth forms being removed; and in that case the posts should be treated in the same way as the college ones.

It would no doubt be best for the new system if all posts were open to unrestricted competition, but this is probably impossible on grounds of cost – too many local teachers would have to be paid even though they had not obtained a post – and because of the antagonism such an arrangement would, understandably, generate among all teachers. So there will have to be a procedure of considering first those teachers from within the area affected by reorganization. This needs to be discussed with the teacher unions in advance and, if possible, a system agreed. Even without agreement, the system needs to be stated in advance so that teachers shall at least know what it is, even if they do not like it.

It is difficult to do much about the balance of gender and ethnic origin. If most of the posts in the new system are filled, as they must be, by people who held posts in the old one, a previous lack of women or black people in senior posts is almost inevitably transmitted to the new system. It is also difficult to see how, without being unfair to individuals, it is possible to guarantee that any one school will not suffer an excessive loss of its best staff to the new college. But what can and should be done is to ensure that the college is not very much more attractive in salary terms than that schools, which is best done by being generous to the schools in staffing, as in everything else, both for this reason and for the more general one of concern for the morale of the schools.[5]

Non-teaching staff often get overlooked in reorganization. They should not be. If all staff of the previous college have new contracts in a new college, this should apply also to non-teaching staff. Failure to do this often causes great problems later, not least because in many authorities non-teaching staff come under the personnel department, and personnel officers can hardly be blamed for appearing obstructive if they have not been consulted in the first place. There will be new demands on non-teaching staff in the tertiary college, and the formulae used in the previous FE college to determine staffing levels will often be inappropriate in the new. A far greater proportion of full-time students, for example, will be applying for higher education and need elaborate references typed on to application forms, necessitating a disproportionate increase in secretarial staffing. While the education department has the main responsibility for setting up the new college, it must not fail to consult effectively the other departments whose support and understanding are vital.

Personnel is one of these; finance another. Just as the college must be staffed according to its needs, so also must its budget be determined and apportioned in full recognition of its changed nature. Yet more than once an authority has officially closed a further education college and opened a tertiary college in its stead only to have, as a result of its failure to involve them, the personnel and finance departments working on the basis of its still being the old college. The results can be crippling, and it can take a vast amount of time – quite unnecessarily – to resolve problems that need never have arisen.

The larger the college, the greater the range of provision that can be afforded. But large colleges are unwieldy and may be impossible to organize effectively as a unity, as well as having too many feeder schools for effective liaison. Furthermore, there is a lot to be said for a college that is sufficiently small for its members to at least recognize the principal and for the principal to have the time to walk round fairly frequently. It is difficult to be specific with any confidence, but I would say that 2,000 full-time students aged between sixteen and nineteen is too many, and nearer a thousand is preferable.[6]

Physical provision

Physical provision is, of course, also important. Split-site colleges should be avoided if at all possible, not merely because travelling between sites is inconvenient but because having more than one site can actually make it difficult to achieve some of the aims of unified post-sixteen provision. Maximizing the number of different combinations of courses and subjects depends not only on timetabling but also on being able to move from one class to another in the interval between classes, and split sites may make this impossible. And if specialist accommodation is on different sites which are too far apart to be integrated into a common timetable, it may be impossible to take a mix of different specialisms such as modern languages with business studies or arts A levels with sciences or A-level physics with engineering. It might, therefore, be essential to provide a transport system between sites.

If the college is fortunate enough, as Halesowen was, to have new buildings or substantial modifications to existing ones, this presents an opportunity to have the philosophy of the college reflected in its accommodation. If the college wants to emphasize that it is not a school, it is obviously a gain if the buildings do not make it look like one. Collaboration between the college, the local authority education officers and architects and the DES Architects and Buildings (A & B) group was very fruitful at Halesowen, and we have college buildings that are attractive, warm and friendly in appearance while also being functional. And the Dudley Authority was wise enough not to penny-pinch, so the building materials and fittings are of good quality and the overriding consideration was not to get the maximum number of people in for the least cost. The subsequent success of the college, and the care with which all college members treat the buildings, fittings, furniture and equipment, certainly owe a lot to the authority having provided a college which is pleasant to work in and in which one can reasonably take pride. The feel is domestic rather than institutional. Classrooms in the new blocks are carpeted, for example.[7]

Whether in new buildings or not, the new college will need substantial amounts of new equipment. It is a mistake to think that the sixth-formers can, as it were, come from the schools bringing their books and equipment with them. For a start, in many subject areas the school sixth forms will have followed different syllabuses and used different books and equipment. Secondly, the schools will not have much that was exclusively for sixth form use. Most of it will have been used by the main school, so to remove it harms the provision for younger pupils. Thirdly, a lot will be in a poor state, not because schools cannot look after things, but because in the years when removal of the sixth forms was pending it would not have seemed sensible to spend on new books and equipment for them if what they had could be made to last a little longer. Trying to get sixth form books and equipment out of the schools is hardly likely to be worth the effort, and any attempt at compulsion will be certain to generate great hostility for little return. Raiding parties of advisers will probably come away empty-handed but do great damage to realtionships. So when calculating the cost of setting up the college, no assumption of inheriting anything from the schools should be made. Whether anything is transferred should be left as a matter between the schools and the college, to the professional partnership that is essential to the success of the reorganization.

Liaison and transition arrangements

Several principals of the tertiary colleges set up in the 1970s candidly admitted to me that one area where they felt they could have done better was in liaison with their partner schools. Not that their relationships with the school heads were bad. Far from it. But somehow the liaison arrangements seemed to bear insufficient fruit. Reflecting on my visits to these colleges, it seemed to me that certain general principles of effective partnership could be formulated. In the light of our experience at Halesowen, I would summarize these as follows.

The foundation of this partnership can be laid more effectively at the time of reorganization than later. The tasks of planning the curriculum of the new college and making arrangements for the admission of students and for the transition period should be given to a committee comprising the heads and deputies of the college and of the schools. Having important and urgent tasks to do will weld the members of this committee together, and when the new system is under way the committee can continue as the overall schools–college liaison committee. Setting up such a committee at the outset will also do a lot to convince the schools that they are not being overlooked in the enthusiasm for founding a new college. It will, furthermore, establish one essential for effective liaison in the future, namely a single coordinating committee to which all other liaison committees are accountable. Obvious though this is, it is often overlooked. Without it, a committee charged with coordinating, say, mathematics will tend to fragment as soon as there is disagreement, with each member reporting individually to their own school or college head, and indeed soliciting their support. If they account collectively to a single body, the chances of this happening are much reduced.

As part of the planning for setting up a tertiary college at Halesowen, the Dudley Authority formed what were in effect two sub-committees of the education committee, called the shadow governing body and the shadow academic board. The former, like an actual governing body, had a majority of elected councillors; the latter consisted of the designate principal and vice principal of the proposed tertiary college, and the heads and deputies of the existing FE college and secondary schools. The shadow academic board was charged with advising on the transition from the old system to the new. This included arrangements for the admission of students, and, as the first chair of the board, I extended this to include drafting the prospectus for the proposed college, and involved my school colleagues in decisions on the curriculum, pastoral organization and the internal organization and discipline of the college. Some expressed surprise at the extent to which they were to be involved, and even reluctance on the grounds that they might be infringing on my professional responsibilities. But when they were convinced I was in earnest, they gave most valuable advice, raising many points that would have escaped me; and the college, when it eventually came into existence, benefited as a consequence.

Remarkably, the bulk of these discussions took place *before* the college was given ministerial approval, let alone opened, and therefore at the same time as some senior school staff were actively campaigning *against* the college ever being set up.

Ministerial approval for the reorganization came in late April 1982, and clearly was a very close affair. The very next day, the head who had been most prominent in the campaign against the proposals sent a circular letter to all parents at his school telling them that the argument was now over and that he would be doing everything he could to make the new system work. The college opened four months later. Without the work done by the shadow academic board and the selfless professionalism of the heads, including those opposed to the reorganization, this would have been impossible.

It seemed obvious to me and the school heads that this shadow academic board should continue as the schools–college liaison committee. Despite unexpected opposition from one quarter within the authority, the schools–college liaison committee came into being, with a school head as its chair. We have since agreed that the chair should rotate every three or fours years, but I feel it should always be occupied by a school head, never the college principal, so as to avoid giving an impression of a 'big brother' attitude on the part of the college.

Having got our overall liaison committee, the next step was to set up sub-committees, or panels as we call them, for the various aspects of liaison. And, crucially important, to specify what they were expected to do. All but one, that on pastoral care, were defined by subject area; and the convenorships of these panels were divided equally amongst the five institutions – the four schools and the college. Each received a letter from the new liaison committee chair charging them to advise the committee on three main matters: curriculum continuity from school to college; sharing of human resources; sharing of material resources. They were asked to meet at least termly and to submit a report at least annually.

Note the wording of the injunction to advise on curriculum continuity. There is no suggestion that the schools should fall into line with college, or vice versa. Rather, the implied assumption is that the panel will work as a group of professionals and will determine what is in the best interests of the students without regard to any consideration of whether schools or college should predominate. A measure of the success of this approach is that not once in five years have I or one of my headteacher colleagues openly supported our own staff in an internal panel dispute. Not that there have not been such disputes, but the panel is responsible collectively to the liaison committee, and individual members of that committee would see it as incompatible with their responsibilities to get involved in panel disputes.

Other signs of success are the lack of any conflict on what syllabuses should be followed, the number of staff who visit and even give classes in a partner school or the college, and a plan to introduce Nuffield sciences (a well-known set of experiment-based courses) in one of the schools using equipment at the college. In all of this there must be an assumption of parity in the relationship between college and school staff. The college must take care always to attribute some of the credit for student successes to the schools, which is only reasonable; students who gain, say, Cambridge entrance will have been in the college for a shorter time than in the previous school. Also as a matter of course, the college should send the schools as much information as it can about their former pupils – examination results, for example.

Continuing liaison is vitally important, as are effective transition arrangements during the implementation of the reorganization.

The main aim of the latter must be to ensure that no student suffers because of the reorganization. Some students in the school sixth forms will have completed one year of their A-level course when the reorganization starts. They must be given the option of completing the course in the school, even though there will be no first year there during their second year. Some of their teachers will have been appointed to the college. To ensure continuity of teaching, they must continue to teach school second-year sixth-formers whom they took in the first year, as well as main school classes where a change of teacher would be undesirable.

Having a number of teachers dividing their time between college and a school requires complex planning and logistics, and is also expensive as a good deal of time will have to be allowed for travelling. But, for one year, it is essential that it be done.

Among other things, such transition arrangements demonstrate the importance attached to the teaching of pupils in the schools. This needs to be reinforced by a policy of ensuring that the schools benefit in terms of books and equipment, and if possible buildings, from the economies of scale brought about by concentrating sixteen-plus provision.

It is not, however, enough for the college to *become* successful; it must *be* successful from the first day. Otherwise, those who are its first student intake will be at risk. This is a legitimate fear of opponents of any reorganization; that it may be right eventually but at the cost of harm to those caught up in the reorganization.

But how is immediate success to be achieved? Assuming adequate material resources, there are two further vital ingredients. The system of reorganization must be properly planned, and the people who will be in the college, students as well as staff, must have the will to succeed.

Learning from experience

In planning any new institution, there must be an adequate period for appointing staff and determining who does what, for admitting students and devising a timetable – and for consultation with all the individuals and groups involved. Nevertheless, this period can be too long. Principals, and sometimes the senior staff, are appointed in advance. But they should not have more than about a year, or the prospect of the new college is too distant to concentrate minds on making it work and, instead, there will be a tendency for petty jealousies and private power struggles to develop. As with impending execution, nothing so concentrates the mind as the knowledge that the great moment is imminent. Unity is more likely to be achieved by a planning period that errs on the side of brevity. A feeling can be generated that there is no time for any diversion from the main task. The possibility of going over the cataract will inspire in all the crew a determination to pull hard. And together. Provided, that is, the helmsman appears to know in which direction to point the boat.

As the inevitable day approaches, positive leadership is called for to get everyone looking forward, however apprehensively. And students must not be overlooked in this, both those who will be joining from the schools and those already in the FE college.

In the four frenetic months from the date the Halesowen reorganization got government approval to the day it opened, the principal designate waxed lyrically at many formal and informal meetings of the future staff. This on its own would probably have achieved little. At the beginning of July, when nearly all knew, at any rate in broad outline, what they would be doing in the new college, a one-day conference for the whole teaching staff and senior support staff was called. At this, I said next to nothing (the novelty must have been striking!). Instead, all the speakers were from outside – most notably Mike Austin, Principal of Accrington and Rossendale College, and Simon Lambert, the then Staff HMI for sixteen-plus. They will, I hope, forgive me if I say that what they said was relatively unremarkable. The important thing was that two people who could speak from experience said much the same as I had been saying for some months. Their authoritative corroboration engendered more belief than I could have done on my own.

As is the wont of conferences, this one divided for some sessions into discussion groups. In these staff from the FE college and from the schools worked together on particular aspects of our plans. And they gelled. A college which starts with FE and school staff in two distinguishable groups is a house divided against itself. And we all know the consequences of *that*.

There will not often be the chance to do something similar for students. At Halesowen there was.

In addition to my addressing meetings in the schools of fifth-formers and of their parents, we ran, with the co-operation of the school heads, a two-day conference for all future first-year students. We used a Challenge of Industry conference, run by the

Industrial Society. The aim of these conferences is to give sixth-formers an insight into the problems and satisfaction of working with others in an organization. The conferences are run entirely by the staff of the Industrial Society.[8]

The Society agreed to depart from normal practice and hold a conference for fifth-formers, and the conference chairman encouraged consideration of one particular organization, the college they were all about to join. At the final plenary session he engineered my being called in to answer questions about the extent to which students would be treated as true partners in the new college. This conference, attended by over half of the first intake as well as by a sprinkling of students from the FE college who would join as second-year students, did an enormous amount to get students positively looking forward to starting in the college. With the overwhelming majority of staff and students in this frame of mind, Halesowen College did indeed achieve immediate success, and there is no evidence that even a single student suffered as a consequence of being caught up in the reorganization.

In any human enterprise success is the product of many factors. Luck is certainly one of them! And hard work and team spirit, while necessary, are unlikely to be sufficient on their own. In addition there must be the right order of priorities, and a sense of a new direction. It is to these matters that I turn in the next chapter.

Notes

1. In the 1986 *Compendium of Sixth-Form and Tertiary Colleges.*
2. Ibid., pp. 136–138.
3. In the 1983 general election, none of the manifestos of the three major parties made any reference at all to tertiary colleges; four years later, all three did, albeit with varying degrees of equivocation. The Alliance planned 'To develop tertiary colleges where local conditions are appropriate'; Labour said 'We will spread the provision of a comprehensive tertiary system of post-school education'; the Conservatives said they supported 'the co-existence of a variety of schools – comprehensive, grammar, secondary modern, voluntary controlled and aided, independent, sixth-form and tertiary colleges – as well as the reasonable rights of schools to retain their sixth forms'. Of the Alliance one could ask what is meant by local conditions being 'appropriate'; of Labour whether a 'comprehensive tertiary system' does or does not mean tertiary colleges. But the Conservatives, by apparently committing themselves to everything had, of course, actually committed themselves to nothing.

4. This is by no means always true. The Dudley Education Authority, for example, was both decisive and courageous during the Halesowen reorganization.

5. In early 1987, there seemed to be an opposite danger, of a pay and conditions structure for schools imposed by Parliament giving schoolteachers a rise of around 20 per cent but with no equivalent increase for college teachers. I am not arguing for this!

6. Halesowen College opened with 661 full-time students and four years later, in 1986–7, had 1,266. Numbers were expected to stabilize at around 1,350 full-time students, with around 3,000 part-time, most of whom were adult–evening students.

7. The DES A & B group publishes a series of pamphlets which they call broadsheets. No. 14 is about Halesowen College, and is available from DES Publications, Honeypot Lane, Stanmore, Middlesex, HAY 1AZ.

8. An independent organization offering training, consultancy and advice to both sides of industry; all the speakers and group leaders, most of whom are under thrity-five, are recruited by them from industry and commerce. For information, write to The Industrial Society, Robert Hyde House, Bryanston Square, London W1H 6LN.

CHAPTER 4

Priorities, aims and relationships

As Sydney Smith, the Victorian cleric and wit, observed on seeing two fisherwomen hurling abuse at each other from the upstairs windows of adjacent Billingsgate houses; they will never agree as they are arguing from different premises.

In the debate before the college opens, much argument is likely to have been from premises or assumptions as different as those of Sydney Smith's fisherwomen. Many statements will have been made as if they are incontrovertible facts when they are at best assumptions and at worst myths: that the tertiary college being under Further Education Regulations means an FE takeover; that FE means the destruction of academic standards as the supposedly lower standards of engineers and caterers undermine the studious habits of A level students; that only schools can provide effective personal tutoring, careers advice and partnership with parents. And, no doubt, a distinction will have been drawn between educational aims on the one hand and economic ones on the other; a distinction that is manifest nonsense as resources are inevitably limited so that the more economic management of them must make it at least possible to spend more on teachers, books, equipment and buildings.

The focus of hostility is likely to be the new college; and this needs to be faced. A first task must be to gain the confidence of those who are against the college and the new system; and the arguments of the opponents must be confronted. A clear idea of what it is that the college is seeking to achieve is obviously essential. But first the college must answer the immediate objections.

The two main doubts are likely to have been about its ability to tutor and to teach A level students. The college must therefore set up a first-class pastoral care system and achieve good A-level results as soon as possible.

The myth is that schools are uniquely good at A-level teaching and pastoral care. The reality is often very different. Although there are many exceptions, schools often do not get particularly impressive A-level results, for the simple reason that most school sixth forms are not large enough to permit effective arrangements for teaching; classes are too small to allow a proper allocation of hours so that the expedient of teaching upper and lower sixth together is often resorted to; and there are not enough well-qualified and able teachers to go round. In most reorganizations, the advantages of scale for the new college, and the virtual certainty of having enough good teachers, make A-level success relatively easy to achieve. However, the first year's intake is likely to be denuded of the academically able whose parents, believing the myth, will try to get them in elsewhere, and care must be taken to compare like with like when presenting A-level results two years later.[1]

Public beliefs about pastoral care are likely to be equally wide of the mark. Before reorganization much will probably have been made of the allegedly high quality of pastoral care in school sixth forms, and of the value of continuity in the same institution. The knowledge the teachers have built up about pupils in the lower school can be passed on as they transfer to the sixth form, but must be lost if they have to go elsewhere. Or so it will have been said, conveniently forgetting that pupils transferring to the sixth form of the same school will almost invariably have new personal tutors. And internal communications in a large all-through school can actually be worse than between an eleven-to-sixteen school and a college where, precisely because everyone can see there are problems, formal mechanisms are likely to be set up to overcome them. Written background information about pupils can be sent to a new institution; the information uniquely available to the school sixth form consists of folklore, rumour and hearsay, and it is far from self-evident that it is invariably to the advantage of the student.

Those who proclaimed the high quality of pastoral care in the schools will also have denigrated, either overtly or by implication, pastoral care in the local FE college, probably quite unfairly, and to the justifiable indignation of the college lecturers. Nevertheless, this is another myth that must be confronted. And refuted. For the tertiary college which assimilates the former FE college there is the complication that many of the staff will have come from the FE college whose teaching and pastoral care have been rubbished by opponents of reorganization, probably from a position of almost total ignorance. Yet the new college, in combating the myth, has to appear to accept it, at any rate in part. Much must be made of the new system of pastoral care that is being set up, and it is probably impossible to avoid implying its superiority over previous FE practice. In fact, the new system is much more likely to be significantly superior to previous practice in the schools than to that of the FE college, partly because economies of scale allow a more generous allocation of teacher time to tutoring, partly because the advantages of continuity in the same institution are mainly fanciful, partly because complacency is likely to have affected the schools' systems. Moreover, many FE colleges are, in fact, often rather good at pastoral care.[2]

Longer-term aims for a particular college, or school, must be derived, whether openly or not, from beliefs about the purposes of education. While schools and colleges have urged on them more and more different objectives, not all of which are consistent or even possible, few would dissent from the propositions that education is a lifelong process and that for young people it is concerned with personal and social development as they grow up in a democracy where individual liberty is cherished. To secure both the future well-being of our society and that of its individual citizens, schools and colleges must aim at the maximum development of each student's talents, and at making these of the greatest benefit to the economy and to society generally and to other people in particular.

Education as a lifelong process implies a community role for the college, of which more later.[3] But first, the duty of the college to its full-time teenage students implies that it must enable them to achieve individual success in examinations and future careers, as well as helping them to become self-sufficient and fulfilled individuals valuing both their own independence and that of others. Justified self-respect is the only basis for genuine respect for others.

Wealth generation and social harmony both demand that we should be better at working together than we have been previously. Individual enterprise and initiative are not enough – the very future of our democracy depends on a better sense of common purpose. This is especially true as we face the stark prospect of accelerating economic decline as the oil runs out. Benjamin Franklin observed at the signing of that great act of rebellion, the American Declaration of Independence, 'We must indeed all hang together, or most assuredly we shall all hang separately'.

The situation facing Great Britain at the end of the twentieth century is, in its way, as perilous as that facing Franklin and his co-revolutionaries. Who could possibly deny that a college for sixteen- to nineteen-year-olds should play its part in getting us to 'hang together'?

A statement of aims

It should, therefore, be possible for the new college to formulate a list of aims for full-time students that stands a good chance of securing general assent, or at any rate of being non-controversial, which, given the ferment of controversy simmering after a reorganization, would be quite something. These aims will include maximizing individual potential, achieving examination success and good career prospects; helping personal development; devising curricula appropriate to the future needs of a technologically advanced society; encouraging individual responsibility and compassion; and learning to treat everyone equally, thereby promoting a healthy economy and an harmonious and democratic society.

Should a statement of aims, having been formulated, actually be made public? Yes; for several reasons, some lofty, others almost Machiavellian. Apart from drawing them up being in itself an improving exercise for the principal – or indeed the chief education officer – publishing them can serve the purpose of keeping their author moving in a reasonably consistent direction subsequently. If officially adopted by resolution of governors and the education committee, the aims then become those of the LEA and will help also to ensure a consistent policy towards the college. This can be particularly valuable after a few years when the euphoria of a new enterprise has disappeared.

The aims for Halesowen College were approved by the education committee a few weeks after I was appointed principal designate and before any other staff were appointed. Governors have subsequently approved some minor but important changes in the wording, 'handicapped people' instead of just 'the handicapped', 'she/he' instead of 'he/she'. In 1986 the fourth aim was amended to specify that no one will be discriminated against because of sexual orientation. Nevertheless, the statement is unchanged in intent. The 1986–7 version is as follows:

1 To provide a centre for sixteen-plus education for the Halesowen area and beyond catering for the educational, vocational and training needs of full and part-time students.
2 To be an adult educational, cultural and recreational centre for the locality.
3 For each student:
    i) to develop to the full her or his desirable potential and to encourage her or him to aim for the highest possible standards of personal achievement.
    ii) to encourage critical awareness and an ability to think for oneself.
    iii) to encourage and develop a sense of self-respect leading to respect for and sensitivity towards the needs and feelings of others.
    iv) to develop an understanding of the society and world s/he is growing up in, and of her or his responsibility for promoting a healthy, compassionate society and a thriving enterprise.
    v) to encourage individual initiative and enterprise.
4 To develop the college as a community exemplifying industry, cooperation, responsibility, compassion and courtesy, where all are treated as of equal worth regardless of race, creed, gender, sexual orientation, or social class, and where special regard is paid to the needs of people who are handicapped or deprived.
5 To emphasize the relationships between the college on the one hand and Halesowen and its industry on the other. In particular, to encourage the development of new courses designed to make education more relevant to the needs of an advanced technological society.

Once the new college has its statement of aims, it should be used very consciously in appointing teachers, stressed in the advance information sent to applicants, with candidates being asked at interview about their understanding of, and commitment to, it. There is a lot more idealism in people than is sometimes assumed, and a good set of aims used in this way can do a great deal to get a teaching staff with a sense of common purpose and fired with enthusiasm for pursuing this purpose.

Equally importantly – and this may be surprising to some – a clear statement of aims can also do a great deal to attract and motivate students. On the more negative side, commitment to them can be presented as a quasi-legal contractual obligation on each student, and the disciplinary code derived from them. More positively, through the aims students can be made to feel equal partners in the college so that it becomes 'our' college, for staff and students alike.

This common commitment will come about only if practice is generally and conspicuously in accord with the aims. For the principal to promulgate liberal aims along the lines described earlier but to appear to take no notice of them personally would be certain to lead to general disillusion and it would have better never to have issued aims in the first place. So the first person who must be bound by the aims is the principal. And no bad thing either. English school heads and college principals have too much power – far more than in other countries. While not advocating central bureaucratic control of schools and colleges, I do think that heads and principals should be required to nail their colours to the mast and then be obliged to stay true to them. Principles for principals, in fact.

One matter on which the view of the college must be very clear is racism. The college must be totally committed to treating people as absolutely equal as human beings, and anything which is intended or is perceived to imply the opposite must be rejected, and as publicly as possible.

There must be no question of suppressing an incident because of the fear of adverse publicity. If, for example, some racist graffiti appears – as it did once with us – I recommend a public statement *and* calling in the police.

The implications of having stated aims are considerable; and while colleges without them can and do develop admirable and effective relationships and structures from which one could infer what their aims would be if they ever got round to stating them, this seems to be putting the cart before the horse, and it is simpler in both logic and practice to start with the aims. For a new principal of an existing college, inferring explicit aims from existing practice and then using the statement of aims to promote further, consistent, development would be an excellent way of making their mark without giving the impression of disparaging what had been done before they arrived. Of course, a certain amount of imagination in the inferring might not come amiss!

A philosopher acquaintance once remarked to me that the

impossibility of framing an entirely consistent set of aims must mean that almost any action by the principal could, and would, be claimed by him to be allowed. I think she is wrong; and I have found my own decisions influenced, and on reflection for the better by having put myself under the obligation of justifying my actions by reference to the aims. But she is right in asserting that the aims would be regarded with cynicism were it felt that reference to them was mere sophistry rather than a conscious attempt to act in accord with their letter and their spirit and with the principles they embody.

There are two main areas where practice must be in accord with aims. The first is in inter-personal relationships, especially those between staff and students. To tell the students that they are to be treated like adults is all very well, but one can be sure that they will, rightly, be quick to spot examples that contradict the assertion. Better never to make the assertion if it is not to be confirmed in practice.

Open management

A second, and equally important, area where practice must accord with aims, is the structure of management and consultation. The sort of aims I advocate imply, unequivocally, an open style of management with real consultation for all members of the college. It is as much a matter of attitude as of forms of organization. Without the right attitudes there will always be something essential missing, however efficient the systems might be; and conversely, deficiencies in the systems can be neglected to an almost dangerous extent if attitudes are right. Good will and common commitment can do a great deal to make a creaking system work. That, of course, is not an argument for inefficiency. The point is that the spirit of the aims must permeate the systems.

In public consultation preceding the setting up of a college a good deal will have been said about staffing structures and management systems. Reasonably enough. But decisions on relationships are even more fundamental. Emphatically, they should not be relegated to the category of things one can determine as the college develops, as initial practice in this area is very difficult to change later.

Open relationships

The questions that need to be tackled include:

How will staff and students address each other?

What student-only and staff-only areas will there be?

What grades of privileges will there be for college members?

What distinction will there be between teaching staff, non-teaching staff and students?

Questions such as these are of much greater importance than is often appreciated. Certainly they are not questions that any new college ought to duck. The whole tone of the future institution will depend on the answers to them, whether the answers be arrived at consciously and rationally or by the accident of what happens in the absence of conscious decisions.

First, modes of address. Clearly they must be such as to square with the contention that students are to be treated like adults and that both staff and students are to be encouraged to think of the college as 'ours'. The modes of address that symbolize this vary over time and from one society to another, and even within one society there is no single norm. Superiors are called 'Sir' or 'Ma'am' in the uniformed public services and by first names in advertising, politics and many successful commercial firms – especially American ones.

I go for first names, and at Halesowen from the outset all college members, whether students, non-teaching staff, lecturers or the principal, were openly encouraged to use first names both ways in all dealings with other college members. Students, and of course staff, now generally, and readily, address me by my first name, and I refer to myself by first name when I write to other college members, whether staff or students. And I do write personal letters fairly frequently; when a student or member of staff has suffered a bereavement,[4] accident or other misfortune, or has done something notable, such as taken part in a college production, attained representative honours in a sport or done some commendable piece of community work. Whether I am writing to a member of staff or a student, the format is always 'Dear Kate' with some variant of 'Yours sincerely, David'.

Those who have not experienced such informality and equality in relationships with young people are likely to be sceptical and apprehensive – not least senior staff and principals. They have

been so long accustomed to formal styles of address from more
junior staff and from students, that they understandably fear loss of
respect. Irrationally though; for if respect were based only on
whether one is called Sir or Miss, it would have vanished long ago
in these irreverent times. It therefore comes as a reassuring surprise
to discover that the respect accorded one rests on firmer ground
than mere convention.

The practice, widespread in FE and not uncommon in schools, of
attaching strings of initials for academic qualifications and
membership of societies to the names of the principal and other
staff on letterheads and in prospectuses should be dropped. It is in
any case pretty fatuous; most who read these lists will find them
fairly meaningless; and possession of degrees, diplomas, certificates
and membership of societies has little to do with our competence as
principals. The practice is presumably more to do with a
combination of vanity, pomposity and insecurity than with
anything else. Nevertheless, if it had no regrettable consequences,
it could be looked on as merely a whimsical foible – like referring to
each other as principal this and principal that.[5] But it does. The
practice appears to be an attempt to set the principal and staff above
the students and others. And that undermines, possibly fatally, the
concept of 'our' college that this book advocates. So use simply
first name–surname in all places, even avoiding Mr, Mrs, Miss or
Ms as far as possible, and if these are used, make sure they are
applied to students equally.[6]

That every student and member of staff should feel that in a very
real sense it is 'our' college is a theme that runs through all the
remaining chapters of this book. In virtually every aspect of the
college this objective should be implicit, and in a few explicit.
Modes of address is one: another is students' meetings. Schools
must, by law, have morning assemblies, although whether this
applies to sixth-form colleges is not clear. A school head who
becomes a college principal will probably heave a sigh of relief at no
longer having the daily ordeal of the morning assembly. Yet school
assemblies often help to convey a feeling of unity in the school, and
it is a mistake to abandon them altogether simply because they
are no longer mandatory, and are not part of FE custom.
Halesowen College initially had meetings for all full-time students
at the start of each college year; now there are meetings at the start
of each term – at the request of the students' union. More is said
about these meetings in Chapter 8 pp. 131–133. The point about
them that is relevant here is that they are addressed by other college

members, including students, as well as by me, and this enables all
students to observe the courteous informality – first names both
ways – that we want all to adopt.

The rest is straightforward. Toilets. What possible argument can
there be for separate ones for staff and students, let alone a special
luxury one for the principal? To any staff who object, ask whether
they expect to find at airports and service stations separate toilets
for over- and under-nineteen-year-olds. At the same time upgrade
all toilets by ensuring there are always such things as toilet paper
(soft, not the harsh local government issue), towels, mirrors, plugs
and chains, soap. If they are stolen or misused, replace, repair or
clear up at once – eventually the novelty to some of having such
commonplaces of modern civilization will wear off and normal
standards of behaviour will prevail. Motorway service stations
have discovered this; and in a college where staff use the same
toilets, it will take much less time.

The problem of reserved car park spaces is simple: don't have
any. If anyone says they need one, reply that if they are that
important to the college they had better get there first! Reserving
parking spaces is, in any case, a futile exercise; virtually impossible
to enforce, a never-ending source of irritation and pointless
disputation, and invariably leading to inefficiency in use of space as
many of the reserved spaces remain unnecessarily empty.
Furthermore, those who object are likely to be those who would
most benefit from a little more exercise. So away with the whole
nonsense and let no college member – except those who are
physically handicapped – have a reserved space!

Whether or not you are persuaded of the wisdom of the degree of
informality and equality advocated above, you must surely agree
that such a style would be harder to introduce except in the context
of a clear statement of aims, and a thousand times harder to
introduce once the new college had been running for a while. And
the style of relationships cannot but have implications for other
aspects of college life.

If it is important to blur the distinction between students and
staff, it is just as important to do so between different categories of
staff. As staff are adult and most full-time students are not, it is
reasonable for there to be staff rooms where students do not go;
and it is necessary anyway on grounds of confidentiality as staff
will sometimes need to talk about students, and notices for staff but
not students do need to be put up occasionally. But there can be no
justification for excluding the non-teaching staff, and it is better to

avoid the term 'non-teaching', with its connotations of lower status, as far as possible. Instead, refer to them as support staff and try to include them in all staff discussion so as to encourage them to feel equal in status to teachers. After all, many will be doing jobs that are actually of greater immediate importance. It certainly is every bit as urgent to cover the absence of the switchboard-receptionist as of a teacher. And the support staff, with the teaching staff, have collectively a responsibility as adults for the general running of the college, including the promotion of the peculiarly valuable concept that it is 'our' college.

One area where the feeling that it is 'our' college can be demonstrated is in the receiving of visitors – inspectors or local authority advisers, officers, educationalists or politicians from abroad or other parts of Britain, local industrialists or others who rank as VIPs. Invite students from all parts of the college to act as guides, so as to involve as many as possible. Brief them properly, and perhaps have a supply of printed tours of the different parts of the college so that they can talk knowledgeably. Our expereince is that visitors like being shown round by students, and students definitely like being asked to act as guides. We never have any difficulty in getting sufficient volunteers for this. Understandably, they prefer to work in pairs, and we usually pair students from different parts of the college, who often did not previously know each other.

And definitely avoid a stratification of reception according to position in the college hierarchy – lunch and wine with the principal, sherry with vice principals, coffee in the staff room with the staff and tea out of chipped mugs with students in the union office. Instead, mix it up. Let students and staff, teaching and support, join for lunch or sherry. And do not fear to let students talk on their own to visitors. We often arrange for visitors to have an hour or so with a random cross-section of students, and invariably they are impressed. It is a worthwhile and pleasant gesture to send photocopies of subsequent thank you letters to all students and staff who helped receive them. Similarly, when senior staff go to schools to talk to pupils and their parents about the college they often ask the student's union to nominate one or two students to go as part of the team representing the college.

The degree of informality and equality between staff and students which I advocate, and the extent to which I believe one should treat students as equal partners in the college, are much greater than is usual. It is not surprising, therefore, that many are uncomfortable at times, including those who are wholly committed to the principle. Students sometimes wish they were not treated as adults with all the concomitant responsibility. Staff will sometimes resent that the principal has the same easy relationship with students as he or she does with them, and that he or she appears to attach every bit as much importance to student as to staff views.

Staffroom gossip will include remarks to the effect that the principal does not support the staff, that in any conflict he will take the side of the student, that he only really listens to student views. The principal needs to be sensitive to the feelings underlying such remarks, and to check with senior colleagues that they are unfounded. Provided they are, he should not be deflected but should take greater care to constantly re-proclaim the principles on which the practice rests and should try to spend more time talking with staff about their work.

College and community

It is surely obvious that a general feeling that it is 'our' college implies a strong sense of the college as a community. The converse is not true, as a community could be a structured hierarchy with those at the bottomconscious only of their relative subservience. Preparation for adulthood in a democracy implies that a college for young adults must have the sort of community feeling that engenders a feeling of equality and equal responsibility.

This is also implied by the aim of developing autonomy, which can only be achieved if everyone is treated equally as a person. An example of this, pointed out at Halesowen by some female students, is that first names both ways between teachers and students tends to remove one aspect of gender stereotyping. The usual school practice of male teachers calling girls by their first names while being called Mr or Sir in return is patronizing and accentuates the stereotypical male–female relationship. This is not true for relationships between female teachers and boys because there is not, in this case, a pre-existing pattern of dominance that can be emphasized by the form of address used. The important fact is that female students *do* feel more valued as people when they can call their teachers by their first names. That, in itself, is sufficient reason for encouraging them to.

The questions discussed so far are to do with the college as a community, and with developing a sense of community among its full-time members. But the college will also use the word 'community' in connection with its role as a centre for the surrounding population, for individuals and employers in the vicinity. This is by no means an incidental aspect of the college's work; part-time students are likely to outnumber full-time, possibly by as much as five or even ten times, and a significant part of the budget and of management and administrative time will be devoted to marketing, planning and running a wide variety of part-time courses.

Nevertheless, to talk of the college serving the community is really pretty meaningless, strong in what it can evoke but imprecise in what is implied. Community is a sort of motherhood concept; everyone is in favour of it and the word itself induces a cosy glow of approbation, but its meaning is vague or ambiguous. In schools and colleges, the word is used in two broad, and almost conflicting ways. The college as a community implies cutting off its full-time members from the outside world and establishing internal practices, rules and attitudes conducive to certain ideals. As in a monastery. The concept is well defined and powerful, but by no means easy to reconcile with relationships with the outside world. The college as a community resource does indeed imply relationships with the world outside the college, threatening the sense of community within the college by breaking down the walls necessary to protect it.

Some colleges and community schools solve this problem by avoiding, usually unintentionally, mixing of full-time and part-time staff and students. They run as virtually two institutions sharing the same facilities; the full-time college by day and the part-time one in the evening. Few would consciously aim for such a separation, although some local authorities do much to reinforce it by separating adult education or youth and community from the rest of education. Such structures may be neat on paper, but they invariably impede the development of the community aspects of schools and colleges.

The tertiary college, as a comprehensive post-sixteen institution, must aim for integration between its full- and part-time provision. Its aims are equally applicable to both; and need to be known and accepted by staff and students in both categories. This can be achieved only if there is a continuum of provision covering both aspects of the work of the college. Barriers between full- and part-time members need to be removed. Full-time students should be encouraged to take some of their classes in the evenings together with part-timers; daytime classes should be open to part-time students of all ages. During the day and evening it should be unremarkable to see teenagers, mature adults and pensioners in the same class.

In addition, there will be classes of pupils from the partner schools using the specialist facilities of the college, as well as much younger children coming in for playgroup, mother-and-toddler groups and crèches. The staff taking all these classes need to mix; full-time staff doing one or two evenings, part-time staff working daytime as well as evenings. Senior staff, and especially the principal, need to spread their time over both daytime and evenings so that there is no sense of evening work being less important or even different.

It is also important that the rules for full-time students should be consistent with what is acceptable to part-time adults. that is why there is a marked absence of school-type rules in colleges under FE Regulations, all of which have substantial numbers of part-time adult students, but not in all sixth-form colleges, which do not. This liberation is not without its dangers. The college does, or should, want to proclaim ideals and encourage certain attitudes, and not merely respond to whatever the public generally happens to want.

The college which has had its aims approved by all political parties and which consistently proclaims them must be at an advantage should any particular pressure group seek to deflect it from pursuing those aims; for it is much easier to object to particular practices, and of course it may well be right to do so, than it is to challenge openly aims of the sort described in this book.

To talk of the college serving the community is generally misleading for the simple reason that few colleges are surrounded by anything that could reasonably be called a community. But that is all the more reason why the college should have community aims, not so much to serve the community as to create one. Put this way, the community aims of the college cease to be pious platitudes and become instead both well-defined and important. The college must attract the public by providing for their immediate needs and interests, and then serve their longer term interests by promoting a sense of community between the various individuals and groups who come or who use the college to meet. The college is, of course, not alone in this, but may well be in the best position to bring together all the others. And if it is clear about its aims the college can, through them, help to create not only a community among those it serves but also a community committed to the same aims and therefore arguing from the same premises.

Notes

1. See also Chapter 2, pp. 16–17.
2. Chapter 6 discusses systems of pastoral care appropriate to a tertiary college.
3. See pp. 61–63.
4. It has, in addition, been my practice, ever since I first became head of a school in 1971, to attend the funeral of any parent of a pupil or student. I believe this gesture does a lot to demonstrate sympathy and support from the school or college, and its value makes it well worth the small demand on my time that is entailed.
5. Especially in the minutes of the Association of Principals of Colleges (APC), the FE principals' trade union, where it is our equivalent of 'brother' in other trade unions.
6. The heading on a recent letter I received from an FE college principal included (with only the name changed): 'Principal: B A Wash BSc PhD MInstP AMMIEE ACP MIAM AMBIM FRSA MCollP to whom all correspondence should be addressed.' And just in case I had missed the significance of the second qualification, he finished his letter

   B A Wash (Dr)
   Principal

   Of the 151 colleges listed in the 1986 *Compendium of Sixth-Form and Tertiary Colleges*, only two principals give themselves as, simply, first name, surname. Another five omit letters after their names.

PART THREE

Staff matters

CHAPTER 5

Teaching and learning

The limits of the formal curriculum are set by the number of teachers and support staff, the money for equipment and books, the buildings and accommodation; and, of course, the syllabuses laid down by the examining bodies. This leaves a great deal of freedom for the college: What subjects and courses to offer, and which are to be externally examined; how the timetable is to be organized; the time allocation for each part of the curriculum and the length of classes; the system of allocating students to subjects and course; the monitoring of teaching and learning; teaching methods. This chapter is about these matters, over which the college has some control. What sort of examinations system would be best for academic and for vocational courses, how the maze of qualifications can be simplified, whether continuous assessment is preferable to written examinations, are important questions, but only passing reference will be made to them here.

Choice and the Curriculum

What should the curriculum menu comprise? And who should do what? 'Never mind the quality, feel the width' is a catchphrase that sounds as if it might have been originated by a college principal, although it wasn't. The aim of providing for all educational needs sixteen-plus encourages the view that the longer the list of subjects and courses the better. This is not necessarily so. Quality is equally important. Furthermore, it is never the case that all combinations of subjects and courses are possible. The important thing, of course, is to provide as many as possible of those that are actually needed; and this is probably not much affected by whether the college offers twenty-five or twenty-eight subjects. It is only when one gets down to well under twenty that one gets into major difficulties of not offering individual subjects needed by some, like a third foreign language, further mathematics or religious studies.

Furthermore, increasing possible combinations of subjects can be at the expense of effective teaching – or, more accurately, of effective grouping for teaching. Taking the example of A levels all the subjects will be put in four, five or six lists (usually known as blocks) so that those in each list are mounted simultaneously. One can therefore take one subject only from each block. Choice is increased by putting subjects in several lists, but at the expense of setting by ability which is possible when several classes in the same subject take place at the same time.

But it would be a negation of the aims of the tertiary college to restrict students to a diet of A levels, or of anything else. That is why there must be a single timetable for the college as a whole, and it must be devised so as to allow mixes of so-called vocational and academic subjects. This is mainly a matter of national need. We suffer, in a way that France, for example, does not, from a tradition of separating out education in the theoretical from learning about the applications of knowledge. Our long history of relative economic decline owes much to this divide, and the need for it to be bridged is now recognized by all political parties. A tertiary college is uniquely placed to achieve this bridging, and it is of national importance that it should.

There is an implication in this that is not always made explicit, because it smacks of paternalism and offends liberal notions about the freedom of the individual to choose. In its general form, it is that fifteen- and sixteen-year-olds, with the support of their parents, will tend to be conservative, blinkered even, in choosing a course of study. Not many boys will choose to study languages or catering, fewer still typing or floristry. Few girls take maths or physics or computing, hardly any electronics, technology or engineering. And neither sex is likely to be attracted in large numbers to courses not generally found in schools, like geology or philosophy, or to unconventional mixes of the academic and vocational.

We cannot direct; but how far are we entitled to steer? Not at all is my feeling. The only verbs I find acceptable are 'attract' or 'persuade'. Starting that persuasion at the age of fifteen is too late, especially in the case of choice by sex. Sex stereotyping leads millions of women to aim too low and, consequently, to end up with less satisfying and rewarding careers and lives than they might otherwise have had; and it also means that the nation is underdeveloping its human resources. There is a critical shortage of applied scientists and technologists, and tapping only half the available pool of ability – the male half – is disastrous. And the conduct of our national life would surely be greatly improved if we recruited equally from all sections of the population, male and female, white and black. Reflect on how many women or black people are leading politicians, members of either house of parliament, top business people or managers, high court judges, police chief constables, or even, more humbly, heads or schools of colleges.

The tertiary college can provide the curriculum range needed, but it needs to recognize that it cannot do much, on its own, to enable students to take full advantage of this range. Changing the pattern of choice means challenging prejudice and social conditioning, and this needs to be done much earlier than fifteen and is even a task more for the primary than the secondary school. That is one reason why the tertiary college should establish some contact, however tenuous, with its primary schools, not merely its partner secondaries.

Admissions of students

Such attracting or persuading as the college can do directly takes place through its admission system, which includes direct contact with future students and their parents or guardians as well as information via prospectuses, circulars and forms. All need to be imbued with the same objectives: helping the students to choose freely and widely, putting prejudice on one side, so that they will succeed on the course chosen. None of this is easy or quick.

The system we have evolved at Halesowen is based on the general liaison with schools – although, with over sixty schools to deal with this liaison is patchy with those from which we take only a few pupils. With the four main partner schools and the half-a-dozen others sending substantial numbers there is liaison between college staff and the careers teachers so that pupils from the third year onwards begin to think seriously about the college. Each November we hold an open day, aimed mainly at school fifth-formers, although some schools bring younger pupils also.

All aspects of the college are displayed with the intention of attracting any with the necessary ability and all parents and guardians, together with their children, are invited to special meetings to hear the principal outlining the opportunities available. The full-time prospectus is produced in time for the open day and each subject area of the college produces its own supplementary information brochure or sheet. Having been stimulated by what they have seen, pupils and their parents or guardians can then mull over written information about what most interests them. And they are, of course, encouraged to discuss course choice with their school careers staff, to whom we have sent copies of all the information available to pupils.

Our application form was designed, and is annually improved, in consultation with our main partner schools. Forms are distributed via the schools or individually, and are returnable by the same routes, starting in February. The form is straightforward; asking essentially the applicant's current course and prospects (this latter filled in by the school), their interests and proposed course or courses – several being quite acceptable.

The forms are received centrally in the college, logged, and then distributed to the staff in the applicant's first, most likely, subject area. A visit, made up of a tour and an interview, is then arranged for each applicant accompanied by parents, guardians or friends. These visits usually last at least half an hour and are arranged to suit those concerned, usually in the evening. They are often interviewed by two or even three staff from *different* parts of the college so that alternatives are fully explored. An offer of a place and a provisional determination of course follows soon after, but further interviews are arranged where the choice is difficult

In August, those who wish to explore something else, either because of unexpected examination results or a simple change of mind, are able to come into college for further discussion. Despite this exhaustive – and exhausting! – procedure, there will still be some who do not find their chosen course or subjects satisfactory, so we encourage anyone with doubts to voice them as quickly as possible after starting in September so that further changes can be made while it is still possible.

Our aim in all this is to get students quickly on to courses that are right for their aptitudes and abilities and to which they feel strongly motivated. Achieving this is essential for high standards of personal attainment.

Breadth and the curriculum

Concern at the narrowness of English academic education compared with that of other countries has been voiced fairly continuously for at least the last thirty years, and few would think it right for a seventeen- or eighteen-year-old to be taking a course consisting solely of three, or even two, A levels, even though some students and their parents would be perfectly happy with this. School sixth forms, as far as their limited resources allow, and sixth-form and tertiary colleges invariably mount courses designed to broaden the A-level diet, usually under the title of liberal or general studies. And the government announced plans in 1986 for introducing the following year a new half A level, called the Advanced Supplementary (A/S) level, with the same aim. Whether A/S levels will attract many candidates, and, if so, whether they will indeed have a broadening effect, remains to be seen. In one respect at least they are a retrograde step. For it is not only A level students who specialize too soon. So do those on many vocational courses. If it is wrong for A level students to be unable to take subsidiary courses in English, mathematics, a foreign language or current affairs, it is surely equally wrong if catering, engineering or secretarial students cannot. The tertiary college ought, therefore, to have a programme of liberal studies covering all its full-time sixteen- to nineteen-year-old students and crossing the academic–vocational divide. Because the college has courses and students in both categories, this is a feasible aim.

We have not yet done this at Halesowen. Our 1986–7 liberal studies programme is for first-year A level students only, a total of about 300. However, its form should enable it to be extended, and we hope this can be done in the next year or two.

A special brochure is produced for the liberal studies programme, with a copy for each participating student. The following extracts from the 1986 edition explain the system.

> You are required to take two courses each half-term. Try to spread your choices as evenly as possible across the four main areas: Arts, Social Sciences, Sciences and Sport, and Support Courses.
>
> When you have made your choice, complete the booking form in full before handing it in. Please remember that you are choosing courses for both halves of the Autumn Term. Just

before the Christmas break you will be sent another form for the Winter Term and likewise at Easter for the Summer Term.

You will have the opportunity of entering the Joint Matriculation Board's A/O General Paper next year. Details will be announced early in the year.

In 1986–7 we ran about 50 courses divided roughly equally between the four main sections. Support courses included effective study skills and bibliographical research, but all essential support courses, such as mathematics for biologists, are arranged outside the liberal studies programme. Our liberal studies programme aims mainly to broaden the curriculum. Only incidentally does it mix students from different disciplines, valuable though that is.

Our recreational studies programme, on the other hand, has the mixing of students as a definite aim, covering around 90 per cent of all full-time students, Sixty activities take place on Wednesday afternoons, including all the recognized sports in the area as well as recreational pursuits such as photography, pottery, and pictorial marquetry, as well as rambling, bridge, cycling, conservation work, electronics and typewriting. As with liberal studies, there is a special brochure, and some extracts are given below.

Recreational Studies gives you the chance to try a new game, activity or interest – or to continue with one for which you are enthusiastic.

All full-time students are required to take part for two hours on Wednesday afternoons or, for the small number who are scheduled for something else then, at another designated time.

Nearly all the activities are for one term only and you can change at the end of each term to a different option. For some *team games*, however, we do insist on a commitment of *two terms*.

At the start of each term, you are asked to choose five subjects in order of preference. Every effort will be made to ensure that you are given your first choice, but this may not always be possible because places are limited. Some students, therefore, may have to wait until the next term to obtain their first choice and in the meantime take part in one of their other preferences.

1. Attendance at Recreational Studies is treated in the same way as that at any other subject on your course.
2. When you have been allocated to one of your choices, you *must* stick with it until the end of term.

A Recreational Studies Forum will be held in the Main Hall at our Walton Site for *All first-year students* on Wednesday, 10

September at 3 pm. All Recreation Tutors will be present and ready to discuss the options they are offering. All first-year students must attend this forum and sign up with the option of their choice. An Option Choice Form should also be completed at the Forum and handed in to the Recreational Studies Tutor after signing up.

Second-year students do not have to attend the forum but should complete their Option Choice Form and hand it in to their Personal Tutor.

We hope you find Wednesday afternoons both worthwhile and enjoyable.

Aiming high

Two features of the Halesowen liberal and recreational studies are prominent. First, they are compulsory and attendance is rigorously checked. In fact, the average of well over 90 per cent attendance is as high as at examination classes. Second, they are not soft options. Whatever the students choose to do, they have to work at. In both liberal and recreational studies teachers are expected to assess progress, using tests and assignments where appropriate, and to report on progress. Progress reports are recorded and form part of each student's profile of achievement. Almost all recreational activities are demanding, whether they are athletic, artistic or creative. Activities are taken by qualified teachers and students have to work hard and are expected to aim at the highest levels of personal achievement and, where applicable, of team achievement. Most find these areas of the curriculum to be fun as well. This should not be surprising; there is nothing incompatible in working hard and having fun!

Commitment to standards is not something that can be half-hearted; it is all or nothing. That is why recreational and liberal studies must be as demanding as everthing else. Students must feel that they owe it to themselves as well as to others to make the most of their innate abilities, and to learn the exhilaration of personal achievement. But we must not assume this will invariably come naturally, and the college must be a demanding, even tough experience, and must check on attendance and achievement for every scheduled activity.

There is a view that what is demanding must be dull, and that any teaching that involves and excites the student is somehow suspect. Yet there is widespread dissatisfaction with what most pupils learn in school, and a lot of the teaching in our schools is crashingly boring. It is, sadly, the case that a fair measure of O-level and A-level success can be achieved by such teaching – by the teacher doing all the talking, including long periods of dictating notes. And often the same notes that have been used for years. That says more about our examination system than anything else, and one hopes that reform is coming.

Teaching and change

But examination success can also be achieved by lively, exciting, involving teaching; and at the end, students will be left awakened, not deadened, by the course. The college must aim to encourage this sort of teaching. How?

An obvious prerequisite is that the teachers themselves should be both well prepared and well organized. The Halesowen staff guide has half a page on the responsibilities of the subject teacher, including the following:

> Teaching includes:
>   following the teaching syllabus, homework and marking schedule as laid down by the lecturer-in-charge;
>   participating with the subject team in the continuing discussion of teaching syllabuses;
>   keeping abreast of the subject by reading, discussion with colleagues and attending in-service courses;
>   taking part in professional discussions with teachers of related subjects in the college;
>   assisting in the development of a continuing professional dialogue with colleagues in the partner schools.

It is, however, not sufficient to state what is expected of staff.[1] There must be a system to ensure that all staff set themselves the same high standards as do the best. The heads of section, faculty, department (whatever the titles or system in use) must accept a major responsibility for this. And when a proper appraisal system is introduced, it must be concerned with helping staff, whether in teaching, tutoring or other work, to perform more effectively.

In a sixth form or sixth-form college, teachers may be able to get away with teaching much the same content from one year to the next – at any rate for a few more years. Or so it seemed in 1987. But not in a tertiary college. The vocational end of the curriculum is changing rapidly, both in content and in clientele, in response to a never-ending series of government initiatives, mostly known by acronyms such as CPVE, YTS, JTS, APT, AIT, RESTART. No doubt most of these will have faded into history in a few years and been replaced by others. Despite my note of cynicism, I do not doubt the necessity for change. And not only in the more overtly vocational courses. We live in a rapidly changing world, and education/training – I use the terms fairly interchangeably – must change as well.

But change is only possible if the teachers are properly prepared for it by in-service training (INSET). By the mid-1980s this was recognized, and new schemes were usually launched with INSET money attached. There are two problems for the college. The obvious one is that the quality of INSET available varies, so the college must be discriminating. Less obvious, at any rate to those outside the college, is the damage that is done to the present generation of students if teachers are frequently withdrawn to learn how to teach the next generation.

INSET funding usually includes money to pay for replacement staff, and the impression is given that this takes care of current classes. It does not. A stand-in teacher, especially at sixteen-plus, is most unlikely to be any more than a supervisor. Care must, therefore, be taken to strike a balance and ensure that the interests of the present generation of students are not sacrificed to the needs of the next.

With these caveats, change, or curriculum development as we call it, is to be welcomed. And even in itself. I do actually believe in change for the sake of change. We shall all, soon enough, be in a permanently unchanging state. Let's not anticipate this while we are still breathing! But, of course, it is important to change in a way that is also an improvement. This is not difficult. Anything human is likely to be sufficiently flawed to make improvement relatively easy. The tertiary college, necessarily infected with change at the vocational end of the curriculum, is likely to find it spreading to the academic end as well. Not that there is a total absence of external stimuli to change there either – reform of A levels and effects of GCSE,[2] for example. The presence of the whole academic/vocational spectrum will make for change that blurs the distinction between academic and vocational, or, rather, betweeen theoretical and applicable.

Developments such as devising and teaching a science course for students from special schools with what is classed as moderate learning difficulty (MLD), or linking engineering and physics, or introducing information technology (IT) across the whole college, all require teachers from a variety of subject disciplines, each prepared to think beyond their own specialism. It is often maintained that staffing structure is fundamental to this. While I agree that a rigid departmental system tends to inhibit curriculum development involving more than one department, I believe that attitudes are far more important. Even in a departmental system, staff who want to will find ways of working across department frontiers. In a tertiary college the organization will not be departmental in the FE sense, but it may as a consequence give considerable autonomy to smaller units resembling school subject departments. Where this is an impediment to staff from different specialisms working together, it is up to middle management to sweep aside petty barriers and bring teams together for particular purposes.

Heads of subject sections have a responsibility to promote the development of their subject, and this is impossible without, in most cases, working with other subject heads. In doing so they will also be helping with another of their responsibilities, namely helping their staff to perform more effectively. For change is stimulating.

Teaching and students

But how is one to judge how effective a teacher is? Any objective measure, by the students' examination results, for example, is fraught with danger. Examination results are, of course, important; but there are more factors than the effectiveness of the teachers and it would be very difficult, if not impossible, to be certain one was making a fair judgement of a teacher on the basis of examination results alone. Only the students are in a position to know, and one cannot ask them. Or can one? Why not? Some senior staff at Halesowen are experimenting with doing just this, and are issuing forms like the one on the next page.

A constructive dialogue between students and teacher on how teaching and learning can be improved is only possible if relationships are such that there is a genuine sense of partnership between students and staff. Students at Halesowen would all agree

HISTORY O LEVEL   MID-YEAR REVIEW

NAME .... TUTOR GROUP ....

(You may complete this anonymously if you prefer)

As we are halfway through the year and approaching the end of the time available for covering new syllabus topics, I thought it might be useful to review the last six months of the course and discuss possible strategies for the remaining three months.

WHICH ASPECTS OF THE SYLLABUS HAVE YOU LIKED MOST?

WHICH TYPE OF LESSON HAVE YOU FELT TO BE MOST BENEFICIAL FOR YOU?

(e.g. discussion/debate, lecture, note-taking from text, filmstrip/TV, field work, document study, etc., mixture, or no preference)

WHICH TYPE OF LESSON HAVE YOU FELT TO BE OF LEAST BENEFIT TO YOU?

DO YOU THINK YOUR LEAST PREFERRED TYPE OF LESSON IS REALLY NECESSARY? WHAT ALTERNATIVE TYPE OF LESSON COULD REPLACE IT?

WHAT DO YOU NOW CONSIDER ARE YOUR WEAKNESSES WHEN STUDYING HISTORY?

WHAT IMPROVEMENTS DO YOU SUGGEST COULD BE MADE TO THE COURSE AND THE WAY IT HAS BEEN PRESENTED?

WHICH APPROACH(ES) DO YOU THINK WILL BE MOST HELPFUL TO YOU IN THE REMAINING THREE MONTHS? (e.g. cover more syllabus topics, concentrate on revision, revision discussion, revision notes, revision practice essays, audio–visual work, lectures, document study, etc.)

with what many have said, that there is no sense of 'us and them' in our college. We are beginning to recognize that this makes possible a genuine dialogue. And teachers who are prepared to enter into such a dialogue, and modify their teaching in the light of it, will be better teachers as a consequence. Better at getting their pupils through examinations; better at preparing them for self-reliance subsequently, for there are consequences for the student as well as for the teacher in there being such a dialogue; better at stimulating a thirst for knowledge in their pupils. They will also enjoy their teaching more, and be more inclined to remain lively and enquiring themselves.

Discussion of teaching styles and methods was stimulated, at Halesowen, by having to consider changing the length of classes in academic subjects. The sixth forms of the schools before reorganization had periods of forty minutes' duration – fairly standard in English schools – while the FE college had one-hour classes. While these were sometimes double or even tripple periods in the schools, most classes lasted only forty minutes. The new college opened with one-hour classes, probably the maximum that would have been acceptable to the students, and staff, coming from the schools.

The need to change this pattern came from an unexpected quarter. The college started on one site, and was expected to remain on one site. But it suffered the fate of many tertiary colleges, popularity. It grew and grew, so that after only three years it had exceeded the figure of 900 full-time students which had been set as a maximum it might reach after five years. Although it had already spent over £3 million on new buildings, the Dudley Authority would have been prepared to consider more new buildings, using the proceeds of the sale of a nearby school building that was being closed. But they were caught by one of those frequent and irrational shifts in central government that have made consistent local authority planning virtually impossible in the 1980s. Without notice, the chancellor of the exchequer announced a punitive levy on capital receipts. So instead of selling the redundant school building to finance further college building, the only option was for the college to use the building as it stood. And where; which is about a mile away and the other side of a major road intersection.

To maintain an integrated timetable right across the college, we decided to try to run a minibus service between the two sites on which we now had to operate, as well as leaving time to walk for those who chose to. With one-hour classes, minibuses would have had to run twice in the morning and twice in the afternoon, with a fifteen-minute break each time. We tried it for a year, and it was very unsatisfactory; not least because the minibuses were driven, voluntarily, by caretakers and the disruption to their other work was too great. The only solution was to have one-and-a-half-hour classes so that only one break would be needed each morning and afternoon.

Academic board debated the matter over several hours, and eventually decided overwhelmingly to recommend one-and-a-half-hour classes. But students, through their representatives, strenuously argued against longer classes, saying that some classes were too long for effective teaching already. Nevertheless, the change was made, but even with a new intake of students, opposition continued. At last it dawned on the senior staff that what was at issue here was teaching methods, and it was revealed that a fair number of teachers did virtually all the talking in most of the classes they took. And their students were quite right to say that their learning was suffering as a consequence.

Students on vocational courses were largely unaffected by all this, although their classes continued to be fitted into the common college framework, because they were accustomed to having practical sessions lasting three or more hours. And even in their theory classes they largely took the change in their stride, for their teachers, although usually keen to be known as lecturers, had never in fact gone in for much lecturing. It was elsewhere that the discovery had to be made that lecturing is seldom effective teaching; whether classes last one hour or one-and-a-half-hours mainly affects how endurable it is to be lectured at, not how inadequate it is as a teaching method for most teachers, and most students. Admittedly, there are the rare gifted performers who can be both enjoyable and instructive in a lecture lasting an hour or even more. A few of us might manage this occasionally, or convince ourselves that we do. But most of us most of the time become boring if we talk without a break for more than twenty minutes. (Discreet enquiry even revealed that I was less fascinating when talking uninterruptedly than I had realised!)

So, thanks to a capricious act of government and the persistence of our students, there has been a general and continuing debate within the staff about teaching methods.

The needs of industry

One aim for a nation's public education system must, of course, be to provide its young people with the skills needed to promote the wealth of the nation. The ever-increasing technological revolution has profound implications for education. The symptoms of the failure of our system of education and training were readily apparent by the early 1980s; skill shortages despite very high unemployment, an appallingly low level of spending by private firms on training, low numbers of entrants to higher education taking science or technology.

During the 1980s the government became increasingly involved in the provision of training and of education. The mechanism was the Manpower Services Commission, (MSC) originally set up by a Conservative government in 1973 as a tripartite body drawn from government, industry and the unions with the aim of improving skills training so that the country could face the challenge of entry into the European Economic Community (EEC).

The Thatcher government elected in 1979 was opposed to tripartite bodies and quickly abolished the industrial training boards. However, far from declining, the MSC grew and by 1985 had a budget of over £2,000 million. But the influence of the trade unions became insignificant. The main instrument of the MSC was the Youth Training Scheme (YTS) under which trainees receive a mixture of work experience and training, with the latter, for ideological reasons, being provided by profit-making private training organizations wherever possible. However, a considerable amount also has to be provided by FE colleges, including tertiary colleges, and the MSC had, by 1987 when YTS was available for all sixteen- and seventeen-year-olds not in employment or education, become a major influence on local authorities and their colleges.

Few would disagree with a continuation of government intervention in education and training, but there are dangers in an MSC-type approach. If training is job-specific, it might meet an immediate need but will virtually guarantee redundancy when technology advances and makes the particular skill obsolete. Skills training must be sufficiently general to facilitate the acquisition of new skills when necessary.

There is another way, too, in which education and training can be rooted in the present, or worse still, the past. The laudable aim of relating training to the needs of employers is by no means easy to achieve. For a start, a high proportion of employers have little idea of what their own needs are. It is not unknown for a training department to train in skills their own firm no longer needs because no one told them. Indeed, given the generally abysmal record of British management, it would not be unreasonable to give less weight to the views of employers. There is certainly no reason to suppose that employers are likely to be any better than anyone else in foreseeing the direction of technological change. Furthermore, many employers, including eminent ones, are startlingly ignorant about the content of educational courses and often continue to demand paper qualifications that are largely, or even completely, irrelevant to the job to be done. The government also wanted colleges to earn increasing amounts of money from selling courses and services to industry. Colleges had, in fact, been doing this for years, and marketing the college, as it is termed, had become of increasing importance. Marketing has two aspects, ascertaining actual or potential demand and using the college skills, equipment and premises to meet that demand. Considerable public capital, both human and material, is tied up in colleges, and it is highly desirable that it should be used as much as possible.

There can also be great benefits, apart from money, in such marketing as a result of staff becoming more aware of the world for which they are preparing their students, and of full-time students coming more into contact with applications of knowledge. But there are dangers also. By no means everything that a college is doing, and ought to be doing, can be sold commercially, and the profit motive must not be allowed to dominate. For example, art, music, drama and dance are enormously important and need to be expanded so as to permeate the whole college regardless of whether they can make money.

One of the main aims of the MSC is to improve the quality of skills-training in colleges and to make colleges more responsive to the needs of industry, the assumption being that they are singularly bad at both. A report from the government's own inspectorate, the HMI, published in May 1987[3] in fact showed that, on the contrary, FE colleges are rather good at providing requested training and at liaison with employers. One might have thought it worthwhile to have done this survey before the MSC embarked on improving co-ordination between colleges and employers. In any event, the MSC completely ignored the report: a senior official told me he had not read it and did not intend to.

If teachers are to provide the education and training the nation needs, they must have adequate time for preparation and marking. Blindingly obvious as this is, it is a point that sometimes appears to escape the administrators, not least those of the MSC. Whatever else it might have achieved, the MSC's intervention has certainly led to a vast increase in meetings, form-filling and the compilation of reports, occupying a considerable proportion of the time and energy of staff at all levels, especially middle and senior management. Most of this is unnecessary, tedious and frustrating, and had little or nothing to do with good management of the college or effective teaching. As they say in Yorkshire, no one ever fattened a pig by weighing it.

Not that the MSC is slow. Indeed, the most usual objection is that, in responding to political direction from above, it seeks to introduce major new courses without considering the effects on provision as a whole or ensuring proper preparation. The attitude seems to be that so long as their forms are filled in the classes will be satisfactory. If the MSC is to remain central government's chosen instrument, there is an urgent need to overhaul its procedures and change its attitudes.

But it is a nonsense anyway to have two central government departments involved in schools and colleges. The Youth Training Division of the MSC should be merged with the Department of Education and Science – perhaps shedding 'science' in the process – to form a single department responsible for education *and* training in schools *and* colleges. This idea was, indeed, mooted in the run-up to the 1987 election with, it was supposed, Lord Young, then secretary of state for employment, taking over post-sixteen education as well. After the election, however, it began to look as if Mr Baker, the education secretary, might succeed in acquiring the youth training division of the MSC, thereby acquiring all education and training up to the age of eighteen, including TVEI. One could but hope he would use this power, if he is successful, to reduce rather than widen the academic/vocational divide. And if he does, he will be acting in the tertiary spirit.

MSC attempts to match training with needs have depended on two sets of data. The first is the result of surveying employer opinion in an area, the second of surveying what is actually done in schools and colleges. Both are flawed. By no means all employers will reply, and any system of classifying courses will have an arbitrary element. In 1987 the MSC launched its Training Occupations Classifications (TOC) on colleges. Every course had to be allocated one of hundreds of different possible labels. The categories were far from unambiguous. Worse, all O and A levels had to be labelled 'General'. Thus TOC described Halesowen College as doing no science. We do, of course, but it is all GCE.

Even if both sets of data were accurate, there would still be two fundamental objections to changing college courses to achieve a match between courses and reported local needs. First, it cannot be assumed that all students will seek work in the locality, and it is not desirable they should. And second, the data on employer needs is necessarily out-of-date, and if one thing is certain it is that the future will not resemble the past, so matching courses with the out-of-date data on employers needs will lead to training in yesterday's skills.

This is not to argue against liaison with local employers, but rather to insist that this must not consist solely of the college attempting to respond to what employers say, especially as those who do attend liaison meetings are often not representative. The real picture might be very different from what is presented to a liaison committee.

It is at least as important for education generally, and for particular colleges and schools, to make employers aware of what is happening in the curriculum and in certification procedures.

Liaison with employers must be concerned with developing a genuine partnership with each side learning about the other. Out of this can come effective and valuable periods of work experience for more and more young people, and emphatically not just those on vocational courses. Indeed, given our regrettable academic–vocational divide, work experience is probably of even more value for those on academic courses. But responding to the needs of employers must not lead to the college doing whatever local employers at the time happen to think they want. In developing the curriculum to meet future needs, teachers are likely to be just as realistic and far-sighted as employers. This is now, however, the view of the secretary of state. In August 1987 Mr Baker stated that it was the government's intention to put FE colleges, including tertiaries, under the control of local industry and commerce.

Not only is there no reason to suppose that local employers are competent to discharge curriculum responsibilities, but there is no reason either to suppose that they want to. Colleges already have local employer representatives on governing bodies, and often have difficulty in getting anyone to serve. Furthermore, there is seldom any mechanism for getting local employers together to elect representatives. It is difficult enough to get representatives of parents in a school, but this is even harder.

Enriching the curriculum

Both students and teacher will want to bring in current issues to class discussion. Many of these will be sensitive, controversial, political. These are dangerous waters. Teachers should be encouraged to explore them, but they need some navigational aids.

One of the first things we did at Halesowen was to invite all staff who cared to be involved to join in drawing up guidelines. An extract from the latest edition follows:

> Sensitive or controversial matters, including political ones, will arise naturally in many different curriculum areas. Rational and balanced discussion of these matters is to be encouraged as making a positive contribution to broadening the perspective of our students and encouraging enquiring minds. The college would certainly be an intellectually stultifying place if controversial matters were excluded. Care must be taken in the treatment of these matters, and these guidelines are intended to give helpful advice and to lay down general rules which must be followed by all teachers.
>
> Controversial issues will arise in many different types of course; examination courses in politics, economics, sociology, law, history and many others, and in liberal studies courses about the world as it is today.
>
> The college aims include the following:
> 'To encourage critical awareness and an ability to think for oneself'.   (see p. 54)
> This aim distinguishes education from indoctrination, which is concerned only with inculcation of certain beliefs. It goes without saying that indoctrination has no place in this college or anywhere else in educational provision.
>
> Teachers should aim to ensure that any presentation or discussion is balanced, with different perceptions, opinions and philosophies each being given fair treatment, either within one session or a series of sessions.
>
> Where the teacher is an adherent of a political party or has a definite opinion on an issue, s/he should announce this, not so that students will embrace her/his views but in order to allow the students to correct for any bias they may perceive.
>
> To achieve balance it may be necessary to arrange for contributions from colleagues or visiting speakers. With visiting speaker be invited who is likely to advocate anything illegal or

education not indoctrination is the aim. That is, they may explain their views, why they hold them and what the consequences have been; they must not proselytize. Nor may a speaker be invited who is likely to advocate anything illegal or who is an overt member of an organization that is illegal or whose aims are incompatible with the aims of the college.

These guidelines proved unexpectedly useful when an Act of Parliament (The Education [No 2] Act 1986) required all colleges under FE Regulations to compile a code of practice embodying specified rules intended to prevent visiting (right-wing) politicians being shouted down or lettings being refused on political grounds. This part of the Act, Section 43, was the product of several last-minute amendments in the Lords, and its wording is ambiguous and confused. The code of practice approved by governors in March 1987 incorporated the guidelines on political, controversial or sensitive matters, and was to a considerable extent derived from them. (Copies of the Halesowen Code of Practice are available from the college).

Departure from the narrow confines of the examination syllabus can, if properly managed by the teacher, bring the subject alive and lead to better, not, worse performance in the examination. Good teachers have always known this, and feared neither digression that follows the interests of the class nor the likelihood of questions being raised which the teacher may not be able to answer immediately. Contrary to the impression sometimes given by those who train teachers, complete planning of lessons is not desirable, and is indeed stultifying. Rather, there should be a general schedule that will ensure proper coverage of examination topics, but it must allow digression into the current and topical. Those who advocate a national curriculum please note![4]

Especially for its sixteen-to-nineteen-year-old students, the tertiary college must provide an educational experience going beyond the formal, examination–determined, curriculum. Precisely because governments largely ignore this aspect of the work of colleges, apparently assuming that being under FE Regulations removes any responsibility for general education, it is incumbent on tertiary colleges to accept this responsibility.

AIDS is a good example. True to form, the DES omitted tertiary and FE colleges from its otherwise laudable educational programme launched in early 1987. At Halesowen we therefore undertook our own. After discussion involving the students' union, the counsellors and senior staff, an AIDS factsheet was produced and issued to all students in September 1986. This was followed up with a series of talks to students and to staff in March 1987 by Dr Martin Wood from the Birmingham University Infectious Diseases Department. These were absolutely factual, and very well delivered. With Martin Wood's advice, a second edition of the factsheet will be issued in September 1987, and he will give a further series of talks the following month, aimed mainly at first-year students, but open to others also. We think we have now established a continuing programme of information on this literally vital subject.

At the same time, and again in consultation with students, counsellors and senior staff, I sought and obtained permission from governors to install condom vending machines in both male and female toilets. One letter in the local paper did attack this as encouraging promiscuity, but was fiercely rebutted by students who asserted that, on the contrary, the college was being wholly responsible. Significantly, although parents have been kept fully informed, including being invited to a discussion meeting, there has not been a single objection from a parent.

Digressions within the class are under the control of the subject teacher. But many highly desirable activities necessarily cut across classes and are undoubtedly disruptive: field study excursions, foreign exchange visits, visiting speakers, sessions on special topics. The more of these there are, the richer the whole curriculum is, but the greater also are the number of interruptions to classes. How are these to be managed to minimize the risk of students' learning being harmed? How is a balance to be struck between the advantages, on the one hand, of steady uninterrupted progress through the syllabus and, on the other, of the enrichment obtainable from excursions and visiting speakers?

I write this paragraph at Lochranza on the Isle of Arran, where I am visiting a college geology A-level field study trip. The week is immensely valuable to the students, but involves missing classes in their other subjects. Some have also recently been on an equally valuable geography field trip and so have missed two weeks of college. And others have taken part in one or more of a wide range of foreign or extended excursions. All that is on offer is intrinsically valuable, but who can say how many and which an individual student can take part in without harming their prospects in other areas of the curriculum? The right balance will be different for each individual, and the only satisfactory way of finding this balance for each student is to leave it to the individual student – advised, of course, by the tutor. Of course it helps if teaching generally is more assisted self-study than lecturing and giving notes to the whole class.

The formal curriculum, whether in classes that prepare for public examination certificates and qualifications or in classes that are merely for interest, should appear the same, imbued with the same aims and taught by the same methods – methods that involve the students in their own learning and demand that they accept a responsibility for it, and are demanding of the students and of the teacher. More often than not, classes will then be fun for both teacher and students.

And whether they are studying cooking or chemistry, engineering or English, accounts or art, the main motivation to learn will be the most powerful one of all: because it is interesting. And often exciting and even beautiful as well.

Notes

1. For a discussion of the organization of staff see Chapter 10, pp. 159–161.
2. See pp. 13n for the examination system.
3. *NAFE in Practice*, HMSO, 1987.
4. In April 1987 both the Conservative Secretary of State, Kenneth Baker, and the Labour education spokesman, Giles Radice, did, while the Alliance spokesman, Paddy Ashdown, wanted only a national framework.
    In the aftermath of the 1987 election the defeated opposition parties were much preoccupied with internal matters. The one urgent external matter was Kenneth Baker's Great Educational Reform Bill – unkindly christened Gerbil by its detractors.
    It seemed unlikely that any of the opposition parties would oppose a national curriculum as such.
    In late July 1987 Kenneth Baker issued a consultation paper setting out his proposals for the national curriculum. It was stated that the new national curriculum would *not* be obligatory for the independent schools, only advisory. Nor would it apply post-sixteen. This reinforced the fear that academic and vocational education would be separated out post-sixteen with the MSC responsible for the latter. Furthermore, allowing schools, including those threatened with losing their sixth forms, to opt out of the local system althogether, which was also proposed, would effectively stop all tertiary reorganizations. And, in the meantime, Mr Baker was failing to give decisions on any such schemes. Some had to be waiting on his desk for as long as eighteen months, causing prolonged uncertainty and continuing waste of resources in the authorities concerned.

CHAPTER 6

Student support and discipline

Pastoral care is the jargon phrase, still not known to most dictionaries, where the nearest meaning is to do with a clergyman's duties to his congregation or a shepherd's to his flock. I doubt whether the tired but admirable men recently returned from the war who taught me in my grammar school days would have recognized it. Not that they did not care in a pastoral sense, but rather that they saw care as separate from teaching. But it was all part of schoolmastering.

The separation of caring from teaching came in the 1960s with the disappearance of the form as a constant unit as more and more options were introduced to cater for ever wider ranges of aptitude. Without a form there could be no form teacher. A new group, the tutor group, had to be invented to ensure that all were gathered together – from such a variety of options that quite possibly no two were taking exactly the same course – in order to check attendance, issue reports, and conduct essential administration. Pastoral care has now almost become a separate branch of the teaching profession. It even has its own association and journal.[1] Yet the unity and identity of the form of yesteryear had great strengths. My form masters were major influences in my life, as I am certain they were for most of my fellows.

It is an irony that the only place in the state system over the age of eleven where the unification of teaching and care has persisted is in FE colleges – the very places whose pastoral care is widely dismissed out of hand whenever a merger of FE and sixth forms to make a tertiary college is proposed. For students on further education vocational courses take not a wide variety of different combinations of subjects, but a course, with a course tutor markedly similar to the form teacher of long ago.

The tutor group

As in so much else, what is needed is a synthesis of the best of school and FE practices. Neither need be disparaged in the process. The unit of pastoral care is the tutor group, whether this group is a subgroup of a course when, for example, the thirty first-year medical secretarial students are divided into two tutor groups, or an arbitrary group of fifteen or so drawn from all the A level students. In the latter case, it is a matter of choice whether the tutor group contains students taking a wide variety of subjects or whether it has as narrow a range as possible. In the former there is no such choice; they are all taking the same medical secretarial course.

It is possible to set up a tutoring system across the whole college with each tutor group containing a mix of students from different parts of the college. Given that one objective of the college is to bring different types of student into contact with each other, there are attractions to doing this. They should, I think, be resisted. The course tutor system has great strengths, and it would probably be a mistake to destroy it in pursuit of a social mixing that may not come about in tutor groups anyway. The option still remains of mixing the non-vocational tutor groups by having, for example, as wide a mix as possible of different A-level subjects represented in each group. This also should be avoided. The great advantage of all the group being on similar courses is that students and tutor start with a great deal in common, thereby giving a flying start to the tutor's understanding of the student and to the relationship between tutor and student on which successful tutoring must be based. It makes sense to extend this advantage to other categories of student, not to destroy it. So, as far as possible, A-level tutor groups should be homogeneous, with, for example, all students in the group taking A-level biology and the tutor being a teacher of biology.

But there are benefits from having a mixture of the two years in the tutor group: the first-year students will learn from the second year about the curriculum ahead, and may well turn to them for help with particular problems; the tutor will always have half the group whom he or she has got to know over the previous year, and there will be a certain continuity in the group. And the group can be extended, with similar advantages, to include students taking related subjects on an A-level foundation course – GCSE for example. Furthermore, many of these students will gain in both motivation and understanding by close contact with those doing A levels in the same or similar subjects.

How large should tutor groups be? How often should they meet, and what for? Group size is usually about fifteen. This does not represent any professional judgement on ideal size so much as the number that gets thrown up by the general average number of students per teacher: national agreement currently (1987) limits grade-one lecturers to twenty to twenty-two hours of class contact a week; local authorities generally allocate staff on a ratio of about twelve to one; full-time students usually have about twenty-five hours of teacher contact a week:

$$\frac{25}{20} \times \frac{12}{1} = 15$$

Under FE Regulations, teachers' contracts also specify an additional one hour in college on non-teaching duties for every two hours of teaching. So one hour timetabled for tutor-group meetings gives one-and-a-half-hours for the tutor to work on tutor group business. Time allocated for tutor group meetings is a matter of balancing available staff time among the competing demands. More time for tutoring must mean less for teaching, and vice versa.

The wide range of tasks for the tutor that I describe later will, at first, seem to require many hours a week. Nevertheless, probably the most that can be afforded is no more than one-and-a-half to two hours. School practice would indicate dividing up the allocation into daily dollops. But this is neither desirable nor necessary in a college. Attendance is checked in every class, so a daily tutor period is not needed for that purpose. Nor need tutor periods begin the day. Indeed, it is best if they don't, as some students and staff, being free for that morning, would be obliged to come in for the tutor period only. It is unlikely that any full-time student would be free for a whole day, and all will have classes either in the morning or the afternoon on any given day, so a tutor period last thing in the morning or first in the afternoon minimizes inconvenience. Twice a week probably gives the right length for a profitable meeting of the group, as well as the best fit with the timetable. For ease of communication, there is a lot to be said for the whole college, or a large part of it, having tutor periods simultaneously.

Teachers as tutors

Without school-type morning assemblies, the tutor becomes an essential communications link, and must pass on to the group generally, and to individual members of it, circulars and memos sent from senior and other staff. The tutor is needed for the completion and return of forms such as those for university entrance, and for obtaining much other information that is required by the college from students – up-to-date addresses, for example.

The central task is, of course, support and advice for individual students in the group. To do this necessitates the tutor finding time to talk to students individually every two or three weeks, and this is a major demand on time. They will necessarily have to establish a relationship with each member of the group, and as a consequence become the person most able to discharge many other responsibilities. Some of these readily square with the tutoring role; others may be felt to conflict with it.

Careers work is a natural part of the tutor's central role; and while I shall argue later in this chapter for the necessity of having a centralized careers service for the college, the tutors must be lieutenants in this service, responsible for ensuring every student is taking the necessary steps to secure his or her future, and for acting as agents of the college careers officer. At least one reference will have to be compiled on every full-time student during their one, two or three years at the college, and there must be a system whereby reports from subject teachers are collated, and a draft reference written.

The advantage of the tutor doing this is that he or she knows the student best; the disadvantage is of obtaining a conformity of style and content when there are so many drafters, not to mention the risk of linguistic solecisms (to put it politely!). The pros far outweigh the cons, but it is essential to help the tutors with what for many will be an unfamiliar task, and to have a system of checking.[2]

For both their support and careers roles, tutors themselves need support. The tutors must be divided into teams, each headed by a senior colleague. There are various ways of doing this, some of which are discussed in Chapter 10 (see pp. 159–161). Whatever system is adopted, teams of tutors – like any other team – should not have more than a dozen or so members; as John Garnett used to say when he was chairman of the Industrial Society: 'If the Son of God chose only twelve, what makes you think you can do better? (And even He failed with one!)'

Most teachers will also be tutors. Their work in this capacity is vitally important, and is, among other things, a major determinant of whether or not students strive for high standards of personal achievement. The importance attached to this must be apparent to all and, for example, being a tutor should not be reserved exclusively for junior staff. Indeed, new staff should generally serve a year's apprenticeship as assistants before becoming tutors. The written specification of the tutor's job in the staff guide needs to be continually revised in the light of experience.

Careers advice

Expertise on careers will be distributed unevenly among the teaching staff, and if all students are to receive the best advice available, some overall co-ordination of careers is essential. Students need information, advice and preparation for making applications and for facing interviews. Some will also need prodding, which is usually best done by the tutor. There needs to be a centrally located careers library where students can drop in at any time to consult careers literature. This should either be near or part of the college library. But wherever it is, it needs to be properly organized, so that everything most students will need can be found there. This is no small task: there is a vast number of publications, and some will walk! The college careers service needs to hook-up efficiently with that of the local authority, and it also needs to provide consultation interviews on request. In addition, the careers service should organize a programme of filmshows, visiting speakers and visits. About the equivalent of one full-time teacher for each 500 full-time students would seem to be the minimum time allocation necessary for all this. And funding is, of course, essential.

The calibre of the careers staff is obviously crucial. The people who undertake careers work, either full-time or part-time, need ideally to have done a variety of jobs outside teaching, to be effective and imaginative administrators, to be forceful personalities yet extremely good at relating to colleagues, young people and employers, and to be committed and very hard working.

It needs to be stated that the college careers service is not a job-finding agency. Its aim, like that of all education, is to help put young people in the position where they can make rational decisions about their own futures. Trying to tell them would be disastrous; we could not possibly have the knowledge to enable us to do this, and even if we did, to have made the choice oneself is essential for future commitment and success.

Personal counsellors

On the same model, should one have one or more specialist personal counsellors supplementing the counselling work of the tutors? Yes; with provisos and caveats.

First, the reasons why the answer is Yes. With the best will in the world, no teacher acting as tutor can expect to have the training and expertise necessary for helping in *every* case difficulty involving an adolescent. Occasionally problems are bound to arise that are sufficiently difficult for the tutor to need help in handling, or which need to be handed on to someone else. Some students will have problems that are, or seem to them to be, horrendously difficult, often inducing despair and even suicidal depression, arising, for example, from failure at course work, severe financial worry, home strife, sexual problems or pregnancy.

To have one or two trained people to whom students (or indeed staff) with major problems can go in the certainty of absolute confidentiality might well prevent a suicide. The confidentiality of the service is essential, and no one, least of all the principal, must know even that a student has seen a counsellor let alone what about, unless the student gives permission. And all students must have confidence that this is the case.

Great sensitivity is needed in the counsellors. Their relationships with staff are also crucial, especially with tutors. They must have a real appreciation of the work of tutors, help to make the tutors more effective, and not appear in any way disdainful of the relatively amateurish counselling of untrained colleagues. They should underpin the tutor system, not undermine it.

At the beginning of each term the Halesowen counsellors come to each of the meetings I have with full-time students, in order to make sure their faces are familiar, and to remind students of the sort of help they give. The students' union contributes or passes on £1 a student each year to a welfare fund administered by the counsellors to help, in confidence, students in special need. It is a registered charity and supervised by a small committee of students and staff chaired by the principal.

The counsellors also distribute a leaflet widely around the college. After giving information about how to contact them, it continues:

STUDENT COUNSELLING

Help offered to those with social / emotional / educational / accommodation / personal / legal / financial / family problems.

Everything you say will be strictly confidential. It will not be repeated to any other student or lecturer (nor to the principal) nor to anyone outside the college

ABOUT COUNSELLING

If you have measles, you go to see a doctor. Why and when would you go to talk to a college counsellor? The answer is: when anything is endangering your success as a student. You must be the judge of that.

When you talk to a counsellor he/she will not have automatic or complete answers but will at least be able to contact other sources of help on your behalf, and suggest courses of action which you might take.

The counsellor's job is not to provide a social service or a 'shoulder to cry on'. He or she is not a 'do-gooder' or someone who gets a kick out of other people's difficulties. His/her job is the practical one of helping you, in a variety of ways, to be a more effective, successful student. This is why you are at college.

The counsellor does *not* replace your personal tutor whom you might wish to see for other reasons, as well as academic matters.

The important point is that there is no need to struggle on letting things get worse or beyond solution.

TYPICAL OPENINGS TO A MEETING WITH A COUNSELLOR

'I can't talk to my mother/father, wife/husband. She/he does not understand'

'I'm not interested in study any more. I can't concentrate for more than a few minutes'

'I always seem to be working but I can't keep up with the work'

'My period is late'

'I feel as though everything I do is wrong'

'We've split up and I feel very lonely'

'My group are visiting ... next month, my parents are not working, can anyone help with the cost'

'I'm worried about my friend. I think she may be ill'

'I need ... for use on my course but can't afford it'

'Can you help me with this form from Social Security'

'I've had a car accident and I'm not sure what to do'

'I would like to go out with friends but my parents won't let me'

Students see a counsellor only if they want to: they cannot be 'sent' to one. Nor are the counsellors ever used in a disciplinary role. With that proviso, they have on occasion been of great help with serious problems between students, most notably when one or more students have been the object of racial abuse from others. But asking the counsellors to help virtually guarantees that no one will be punished subsequently.

At first the counsellors, on grounds of confidentiality, did not keep anything except purely private records. Now, however, recognizing that if one of them was suddenly removed, by the proverbial bus for example, it could be vitally important that others should pick up where they had left off, they do keep records in college of all their meetings with students, and with staff. But these are not part of the college files, and no one apart from the counsellor concerned has ever seen them. And we hope that no one ever will.

What about having a college chaplain? Many dioceses are glad to enter into an arrangement whereby a clergyman is seconded as chaplain, usually with the college paying for his hours in the college. The obvious role for a chaplain is that of counsellor, yet if he (and observe that the chaplain will invariably be a he) is visibly a clergyman, he will deter some from coming to him as a counsellor. But if he plays down that he is a clergyman he will not be a chaplain. As an agnostic I hesitate to advise the Church on this, but it does seem to me that membership of the Church is more likely to be increased by a clergyman/counsellor *not* advertising that he is a clergyman. 'By their fruits ye shall know them' (Matthew 7: 20).

But there is a fundamental objection to having a college chaplain at all. It is that we live in a multi-cultural and multi-faith society, and having a Christian chaplain, however ecumenical and tolerant he might be, would be bound to communicate to Moslems, Hindus and others that their faiths are held in less high regard. Furthermore, it is of the greatest importance for the future of our society that black youngsters should take up educational opportunities to the full, and that whites should have substantial numbers of non-whites working alongside them in all our colleges. Having a white Anglican chaplain is hardly likely to encourage non-white, non-Christian applicants.

Does it follow that the college should have no formal connection with the established Church, the Church of England, as well as none with any other Church? I think it does; and perhaps the college should avoid even having a specifically Christian carol service at Christmas.

Student discipline

Returning to the work of the tutor: what part should they play in student discipline? Some of the best tutors will argue that a disciplinary function conflicts with their caring, supporting image. They are wrong, for two reasons. First, the only disciplinary system worth having is one whose aim *is* to care for and support students; and second, if the tutors do not have a disciplinary function there will presumably have to be another group of staff who do, but who do not care and support – like ushers in Victorian schools.

A disciplinary systems, of course, has two parts: rules and punishments. Both need to be considered in detail before the college opens – they are an appropriate matter for joint discussion with the future partner schools – and both need to be amended almost continuously in the light of experience. In consultation, of course, with the students through their union.

Compared with schools, discipline in the college will probably seem easy. College is not compulsory, all the students presumably want to be there and, furthermore, are following a curriculum of their choice. Certainly staff are not likely to find anything to compare with taking 3b on a wet Friday afternoon – and staff in the college should never forget just how exhausting teaching in a school can be. Snide remarks about the relatively short hours worked by schoolteachers are certainly neither politic nor justified. Teaching in a college is very hard work, but that peculiarly debilitating experience of keeping in order a class of boisterously uninterested thirteen-year-olds is mercifully absent – although with the leaving age being, in effect, raised to eighteen, something like it may surface in colleges.

Fewer rules are needed anyway in the college; with all students over sixteen and a determination to treat them like adults, the aims of the college and common sense can decide most matters. Moreover, the presence of older students who are in their twenties, thirties or beyond, has a very beneficial effect on the atmosphere of the college and tends to reduce adolescent high jinks. For example, dress and appearance for most students should be unlikely to become a disciplinary matter as there need be no general rules at all, except conformity with the laws on hygiene, racial incitement or decency. For parts of the college, like engineering or catering, or for visits, there may well be specific rules laid down on dress and appearance, and the penalty should simply be exclusion from that class or visit. But in general, let students wear their hair any way they please, and certainly don't have anything as fatuous as a ban on jeans!

The Halesowen handbook has the following section, entitled 'Obligations of College Membership'.

The basis of being a member of our college is acceptance of the college aims.[3] So do please read them carefully.

Aim number four is particularly important and describes behaviour towards other college members and outsiders. Note that 'all are treated as of equal worth …' etc. This is fundamental. We welcome everyone here who wants to come and, in particular, every student is equally important to the college, regardless of background, ethnic origin, gender, sexual orientation, course or any special disadvantage.

We work on the assumption that all college members are adult and want to be treated as such, are equal as people, and equally committed to good relationships. Therefore, special privileges are minimal: there are no separate staff toilets or car park spaces, for example. Staff will normally call students by their first names and often prefer students to call them by theirs – as I do. However, in some sections of the college, most notably catering, a degree of formality is required in the industry students are being prepared for, and first names will not be used in class.

Second, courtesy is expected of all college members to everyone else – students, support staff, teachers and visitors; and friendliness must never become discourtesy.

New members will have noticed that I often refer to 'our' college. This is because there is a feeling here that the college does really belong to us all, whether students or staff.

Attendance

Attendance is something that there will need to be rules about. What should they be? School and FE practices seem very different; schools often requiring that sixth formers be off the premises only with permission or if they sign a book, and sometimes insisting that all or some free periods must be spent in supervised private study; FE colleges doing none of these and leaving students free to choose what to do when not being taught. Yet schools check attendance only once or twice daily, while FE colleges do so at every class.

The most defensible part of the school practice would seem to be in insisting on supervised private study, and parents will probably urge this when the college is being set up. Yet does it achieve anything? Perhaps for the minority who would otherwise slack. But what about the majority who are motivated to work by their own determination or by the demands of their teachers? Why should they be compelled to work at a time and place not of their choosing? It must be wrong to penalize the well-motivated for the sake of the ill-motivated. Furthermore, if private study is voluntary, there will be no need to have staff supervision of the private study areas; if it is not, even having staff supervision will not guarantee quiet.

It is not in the interests of the majority of students aged over sixteen to tell them where or when they should do their private study; but the college does have a duty to see *that* they are doing it. The first requirement is for teachers and tutors to check that students are attending classes and doing assignments; the second is to check that the teachers and tutors are actually doing this checking, and not to work on the cosy assumption that all will do this as a matter of course. They might, but it is certainly conceivable that some might be less than punctilious.

If students are not to be compelled to do supervised study when not being taught, there seems little point in seeking to keep them on the premises at these times. So they should be free to be on or off the campus;and there is little point either in having them sign out when they leave.

In the college there needs to be a variety of different places for students, and indeed staff, when they are not in class; study areas, both silent and non-silent – for it is often best to work with others – cafeteria and coffee lounges, games rooms. Several small spaces are much better than one or two large ones. And why not let students into classrooms when they are empty? The only exceptions would be on safety or security grounds in such places as practical rooms and laboratories.

Should attendance at classes be optional? I would certainly square with the view that students must take responsibility for their own learning. But attendance is not considered optional for staff, so why should it be for students? Furthermore, a college that advertised its classes for full-time teenagers as being optional would probably get into difficulties with its education authority. I suspect that the only choice the college has is over how rigorously it follows up absence.

An alternative approach is to argue not so much that attendance is compulsory but that if the college is giving sixteen-year-olds considerable responsibility for planning their own routine, it has a duty to monitor how they are using that responsibility, and to advise them when it might seem necessary. And it must be the tutor who gives this advice.

Getting the necessary information on attendance to the tutor is important. The simplest system is for every teacher at the end of every class to complete a slip for any absent students and send the slip to the tutor at once. This is easier said than done. To the busy teacher it is all too tempting to leave the absence slips until later and then risk forgetting them altogether. It does not need this to happen very often for the system to break down. There are alternative systems involving centralized checking of registers by administrative staff, but they will not be as quick as the direct teacher-to-tutor one. So it is worth persevering with and chivvying constantly to get it to work as well as possible. The complaints of tutors over not getting absence slips can help a lot, as most teachers are also tutors!

What action should be taken if a student misses a class? A fairly common practice now, in school sixth forms as well as in colleges, is to require the student to give a written explanation to the tutor. This is right. Having to write a note puts the student to a little inconvenience and, more importantly, emphasizes that they now have a much greater personal responsibility than at school. At the same time, accepting the student's explanation and taking no further action avoids making mountains out of what are mostly molehills. Some skiving will no doubt go undetected – but then some would anyway. On the other hand, a system based on trusting people encourages honesty not the opposite.

An exception has to be made for absence from tutor period or absence can go unexplained for weeks. So when a student misses a tutor period a letter should be sent to them at home, asking for an explanation to be sent by return. For students under eighteen, a copy can be sent to parents. This has the effect of encouraging students who are ill to get a message to their tutor before the next tutor period.

Reports and parents

Under the age of eighteen the student is still a child in law and it is clearly right to keep the parents[4] informed about how they are doing at college. So we, like most tertiary colleges, do send reports and have parents evenings just as schools do. But to emphasize the responsibility we want the student to accept, reports are shown first to the student who is asked to write her or his own comment on a special slip before all the slips comprising the report are sent, via the student, to the parent. There is an acknowledgement and reply slip for the parents, and we do check that the reports are delivered. When students reach eighteen, the same procedure continues unless the student asks for it not to. For those who join as full-time students over eighteen, the same system is used except that reports go to the student and it is up to him or her whether these are passed on to parents, and whether parents are invited to consultation evenings.[5]

The system of reporting progress establishes a pattern for disciplinary matters. Under eighteen, for minor matters, such as lateness or absence, parents are not informed at once, but the total number of such transgressions is entered on the reports. For anything more serious, parents are involved just as they would be by a school, sometimes by being sent a copy of a letter to the student, sometimes by being written to directly. At eighteen the student is adult, yet the parents may still have a financial interest and the college has a moral, if not a legal, responsibility to them. But what if the student specifically asks that their parents should not be involved in any circumstances? Between sixteen and eighteen the position is clear enough when the parents accept a responsibility for their children, but in cases when the parents break with a son or daughter it appears to be impossible to compel them to be responsible.

At eighteen it is best to deal directly with the student unless s/he asks for parents to be involved. If the student is living with parents – or anyone else – and they are clearly supporting the student financially, it seems reasonable to send copies to them of letters to the student, but informing the student that this is being done.

Supervision of college

What about supervision of students around the college? Schoolteachers accept a general responsibility for supervising the out-of-class behaviour of the pupils – or at any rate the younger ones – as well as accepting supervision specified by rotas. Supervision rotas seem inappropriate to the adult atmosphere of the college – whether FE, tertiary or sixth-form – yet it is idle to pretend that sixteen- and seventeen-year-olds will invariably behave impeccably, or even acceptably. Yet it is out of the question to set up a perfect system in a college: seventeen-year-olds might be able to police fourteen-year-olds, but certainly not sixteen-year-olds.

The college may also have a problem with outsiders, ranging from pupils on holiday from a nearby school being silly, to alienated youths intent on causing mayhem. The latter can be a major nuisance in urban colleges and some have been driven to appointing security guards.

So some staff supervision is necessary, but not school-type rotas. It is a good idea to divide up the premises with each part under the general supervision of a senior member of staff – a vice principal or assistant principal or equivalent. Secondly, with good will from the staff, a good deal of 'accidental' supervision can be arranged – staff choosing to walk through a troublespot on their way to and from classes for example. But perhaps most important of all, the principal and other senior management staff need to leave their offices and walk around frequently, deliberately choosing problem areas and places they have not been to recently. Incidentally, they can do a good deal of useful work with staff at the same time – and it is anyway essential to the sort of college described in this book that the principal and vice principals should not be faceless bureaucrats, never seen by ordinary college members.

The attitude to outsiders, even the alienated youths, is

important. Provided one has not yet reached the position of needing security guards, they should be approached in a friendly manner – by the principal preferably – and not immediately ordered off the premises. If possible, invite them to stay for a cup of coffee in a cafeteria, while perhaps explaining that pressure on facilities does not allow for them using such things as pool tables. Ask about them, tell them about the college and, in the best FE tradition, try to enrol them! And, of course, introduce yourself first in a relaxed and non-pompous way. If one or two are hoping to see a girl- or boyfriend, let them wait by all means; and it is a good idea to tell all students that they are welcome to invite friends on to the campus but must try to make sure they behave sensibly.

I don't claim this approach will always work, and I know that some colleges in the centre of towns have much greater difficulties than I have experienced, but it is certainly worth trying first.

Smoking and drinking

Lamentably smoking is legal and likely to remain so, despite being easily the most dangerous drug around in terms of the numbers it kills. If I could, I would make smoking on educational premises illegal for anyone, including education officers and governors. Failing that, I would like to be able to prohibit it totally for members of staff. I cannot do that either. While I should certainly be very pleased if no student smoked, to prohibit smoking for students while allowing it for staff seems to me hypocritical, and certainly inconsistent with the general ethos of the college. It would also be ineffective. What school has ever stamped out smoking round the back or in the toilets? So the only policy seems to be to allow smoking but discourage it. The best way to be discouraging would be for no member of staff to smoke, and at risk of offending a number of my colleagues who are admirable in every other respect, I do consider it irresponsible for them to smoke in college.[6]

Although alcoholic drink is not considered by doctors to be an invariable health risk, as cigarettes are, it is nevertheless expected that there should be a prohibition on informal, unsupervised, student drinking on the premises. And quite right too. But it seems right, at any rate to me, to allow or even invite students, to drink in moderation under supervision – sherry with a guest or a glass of wine in the restaurant. This seems unlikely to encourage the very great evil of excessive drinking, which in young people undoubtedly is a major cause of death and injury in road accidents. Indeed, by encouraging moderate social drinking, it may actually lessen the chance of excess elsewhere.

Towards the end of the Halesowen handbook there is a section on 'Rules'. Like the previously quoted 'Obligations of College Membership', it is worded so as to be applicable to both staff and student members of the college, an important point. An extract is given below:

> We try to have as few rules as possible; the college aims and common sense being a sufficient guide for most matters. But we do have some general rules and they are given below. In addition everyone must of course obey official notices and any further rules published separately.

(1) STUDENT ATTENDANCE

Attendance is compulsory for scheduled classes, including tutorials and liberal and recreational studies. A register is taken at each class and absences passed on to tutors.

If possible, students must ask in advance for permission to be absent, and explain promptly all absences by a written note to the tutor. For students under the age of eighteen, the tutor may ask for confirmation from parents or guardians (usually informing the student this is being done). A medical certificate may also be required for longer absence due to illness, and is always required for absence from a public examination.

When they have no timetable commitment, students are free to be on or off site, and may choose whether to work in the library or study room or to be in one of the common room areas or elsewhere, provided others are not inconvenienced.

(2) DRUGS

Illegal drugs are totally banned, and any association with their use or sale would be grounds for expulsion.

Alcoholic drink may not be brought into or consumed on the premises, except with official permission for special functions. Nor may anyone be present who clearly has been drinking or is under the influence of alcohol.

Smoking is allowed only in private offices, the staff common rooms, the designated areas of the Block O refectory, the Walton student common room and out-of-doors.

Smoking is NOT allowed anywhere else. In particular, smoking is forbidden in any teaching room or any room being used for teaching, the entrance foyers, corridors, changing rooms and toilets.

In addition, no one may smoke in a college minibus at any time.

The same rules apply to all other forms of nicotine.

(3) EQUIPMENT, FURNITURE, PROPERTY AND BUILDINGS
Equipment, furniture, property and buildings must be properly looked after. Accidental damage must be reported at once. Misuse of property or failure to report damage are disciplinary offences.

(4) THE POLICE AND CRIMINAL ACTS
It is our policy to report to the Police any suspect crime involving the college, including such things as theft or damage to property on the premises, and to assist the Police in any subsequent enquiries, including agreeing to any prosecution they may wish to bring. This would not preclude internal disciplinary measures also being taken.

Sanctions

Enough of rules; what of punishment? School-type punishments – lines and detentions – are clearly inappropriate. Instead there needs to be a discipline system modelled on good practice in the adult world. And that should include drawing up the code of procedures in consultation with the students' union as well as the academic board before submitting it to governors for ratification. And as with the students' union constitution, it should be revised frequently, and for the same reasons. A distinction needs to be made between action taken because of academic failure and that taken because of misbehaviour. The system must have several gradations of response – the intention is to avoid if at all possible getting to the final sanction of expulsion. The only other general point I make here is that all students, and staff, need to be aware of the existence of the code of disciplinary procedures and an outline needs to be published in a readily accessible form.

At Halesowen we have had for some years now, as in fact is required by the articles of government, a separate document entitled 'Student Disciplinary Procedures', and a summary is given in the handbook, with which this chapter concludes.

The college does not have any punishments in the school sense. All students are here voluntarily and any student can ultimately be expelled, but only by involving the governors. A brief outline of the suspension and expulsion procedures is laid down in the articles of government (the legal constitution of the college); and a more detailed student disciplinary procedure has been approved by governors. Copies are available in the students' union office, the library and, on request, from the college office or a tutor.

The following is a brief summary:

Students may become subject to disciplinary procedures for one of two major reasons (a) misconduct, (b) problems with work. There is a graduated series of measures. For serious matters one or more stages can be missed out.

1. Unofficial Warning. Given by a teacher. Not recorded on the student's file. May be reported in a letter to parents or guardians of a student under the age of eighteen, but without a copy of the letter on the student's file. The student may be required to undertake supervised private study.

2. Official Warning. Can be given only by a deputy head of faculty or above.
   a. Verbal Warning. Recorded on student's file and an official letter sent to parents/guardians if student is under eighteen.
   b. Written Warning. As for verbal warning, but letter more explicit and action requested of student specified in conjunction with an official warning. A student may be temporarily suspended from specified privileges or use of facilities.

3. Suspension and Expulsion for Misconduct. The principal (or acting principal) may suspend a student from all or part of their course for up to four complete college days without referring the matter to a disciplinary committee, which is made up of two staff and two student representatives, chaired by a non-voting assistant principal. However the student may insist on referral.

   Longer suspension or recommendations for expulsion must be referred by the principal to a disciplinary committee. Suspension of any length must be reported promptly by the principal to the chair and clerk of governors and to the president of the student union.

4. Expulsion for Academic Failure. The Academic Board may require a student to withdraw from the college because of

academic failure.

In addition, a student who causes or is responsible for damage may be required to pay some or all of the cost of repair or replacement.

At every stage in a disciplinary procedure, a student may be accompanied by a representative from the students' union or someone else. The student liaison officer is also always available to help with any student problems, including those involving disciplinary action.

At any stage the student concerned can appeal the decision to the person or body concerned with the next stage and ultimately to the board of governors.

Notes

1. *Pastoral Care in Education* is published three times a year by Basil Blackwell for the National Association for Pastoral Care in Education. Enquiries about NAPCE to Peter Lang, NAPCE, Education Department, University of Warwick, Coventry.
2. An extract from the Halesowen briefing papers is given in Chapter 9, pp. 153–154.
3. See Chapter 4, pp. 54 for the Halesowen aims.
4. For brevity, parents is used to include guardians.
5. For guidelines to staff on writing reports see Chapter 9, p. 153.
6. Senior staff who smoke in their own offices also detract from their efficiency as a consequence. Non-smoking colleagues will avoid their offices as far as possible and will often find smoking in meetings to be unpleasant or even nausea-inducing.

PART FOUR

Staff and students

CHAPTER 7

The college as an open society

On the scale of openness Britain ranks somewhere between South Africa and Sweden. Concern about the amount of secrecy is to be found in all political parties and is increasing, and it does not seem likely that the anti–libertarian decision of the Law Lords in the *Spycatcher* affair will reduce this, concern.[1] In any event, the tertiary college should be helping to bring about a more open and democratic society, and should itself exemplify an open society. References and files are litmus tests for the college in this.

Consider the reference. There can be few who do not view with apprehension the prospect of someone else writing a reference on them. One's future can depend on it and it is written from a position of slender personal knowledge but which will be treated as authoritative.

What does the boss really think of me? And how do they know? Can I see the reference? And can I challenge it if I think it is wrong or biased?

Files are even worse. In most cases, we can only guess that they even exist. And if we do know of them, can we see their contents? What is in them, and how might they be used?

If the college is to be open, the treatment of references and files is crucial. References are usually described as confidential; yet who can say what confidential means in this context? Does it mean they will not be shown to the person about whom they are written; or that the person to whom they are sent will not pass them on to anyone else? And if one shows a 'confidential' reference to the person concerned, is one obliged to tell the person to whom it is sent?

The two important points are, surely, that a reference should be used only for helping with selection and should never be passed on to, or have its contents disclosed to, anyone not involved in that selection; and secondly that the writer of the reference should be candid and honest. If the writer's candour and honesty are unaffected by showing the reference to the person about whom it is written, surely there can be no objection to this being done; nor should the writer feel an obligation to tell the person to whom the reference is sent that this has been done, although should do so readily if asked. But I must confess that I feel less certain about this than about many other things, and I wish there were a clear general convention.

Allowing access to references does have one definitely beneficial effect; it imposes a discipline on the writer to do a thorough job, whether it is a staff or student reference, for the principles are the same although there will be differences in procedures.

Staff references

It is commonly supposed that there is no staff appraisal system in education. But a good reference compilation procedure is just that; it would need only to be done regularly for all staff for it to be called appraisal. For it must involve the subjects themselves and their immediate superiors, a dialogue between them, and the right to see and challenge what is written – although, in the case of a reference this should not, in general, be done until after it has gone or there is a risk of bartering about the reference between the subject and the author. This means that challenging a reference can only affect the next one. But the subject should be made aware of the general degree of support the reference will be giving, even though not, usually, allowed to see it before it goes.

The exception is when the reference is to include a distinctly unfavourably comment. It is, lamentably, quite common to omit any remark referring to an unsatisfactory aspect of the subject's performance. The reader is expected to read between the lines and infer that any omissions are deliberate and because the comment would have had to have been unfavourable. And, it must be admitted, it is not unknown for a good reference to be written on someone the principal wants to get rid of. This is indefensible, and not least because the subject is entitled to know of criticisms from their superiors. How can one improve if one is not told? But, of course, the criticisms might be erroneous. That is why they need to be shown to and discussed with the subject before the reference goes. And the more damning the criticism, the greater the need to reveal it. If, after discussion, which might well be painful, it still stands and the reference is sent containing it, it may well finish any chance the subject had of getting the job. So be it. They may not have got it anyway. It is more important to be honest and to give the subject the chance to redeem themselves in the eyes of their superiors and, perhaps, get a merited promotion later.

The Halesowen system for staff references is described below.

On receiving a request for a major reference on a colleague for whom there is no up-to-date reference on file, I send the following form to the person on whom a reference has been requested. To make matters clearer, I have filled in some imaginary details.

From: The Principal
To: Amanda Digweed
I have been asked to supply a reference on you for the post of Lecturer Grade II in Business Studies at Limeswold College of Technology.

   I intend asking Bridget Smythe and Fred Beaman to provide me with notes to assist on the compilation of the reference, providing they do this on the understanding that you will be made aware of the substance of their comments. Please let me know at once if you have any objection to my approaching these colleagues and please let me know the names of any other staff you would like me to approach.

   In addition, could you please let me have a brief note of recent work and achievements that you think might be worth mentioning in a reference. If you are called for interview, please let the senior secretary or me know at once, so that I can ensure the reference gets there in time.

As soon as this is returned, my secretary sends forms to each of those who are nominated to supply notes, attaching copies of the additional information sent about the job. The form looks like this:

From: The Principal
To: Bridget Smythe
I have to compile a reference on Amanda Digweed for the post of Lecturer Grade II at Limeswold College of Technology.

   I should be grateful if you would let me have, as quickly as possible, brief notes to help me in the compilation of this reference. I have received her permission to make this request.

Will you please be sure that she is made aware of the substance of your comments to me.

Thank you.

When these are returned, they are passed to me, together with the letter requesting the reference and the subject's notes, and I then compile the reference and it is sent. My secretary keeps an eye on the date by which the reference is requested, and nudges people if we look like missing the deadline.

All this takes time. Four working days is about the minimum; and it is objectionable to ask for references to be returned in less than a week. With well over a hundred teaching staff alone, one cannot possibly do justice to a colleague without such a procedure.

It is especially objectionable to ask for comments to be given over the telephone. Such comments are necessarily uncheckable; and secrecy always arouses suspicion, naturally enough. And no time at all is allowed for the proper formulation of comments.

If the telephone enquirer is insistent and refusal looks like being harmful to the colleague concerned, all that can be done is to agree to phone back later and use the time available to get permission from the colleague to comment over the telephone – without permission nothing should be said – and to get quick comments from other staff to help formulate the report to be given. Notes of what is said should be kept and made available to the colleague concerned in the same way as copies of references.

The copy of the reference should not be given to its subject; that would risk its being used subsequently as a testimonial despite the fact that one might wish to alter it. Instead the subject should be allowed only to read it. But not with its author standing over; if the reference is a good one, the subject feels obliged to mumble some expression of gratitude. And that is wrong. References should be accurate; and if one is favourable it must be because the subject deserves it, and the author of it is doing no more than their duty. Instead, copy references should be lodged with someone else – the chief administrative officer or senior secretary – who will allow colleagues to read references but not take them away and will *not* tell their author even that this has happened. And, of course, the person concerned needs to be informed when a reference has been sent and that a copy may be seen.

We send the following memo to the colleague when the reference is posted:

From: The Principal
To: Amanda Digweed

I have today signed a reference on you for the post of Lecturer Grade II at Limeswold College of Technology.

You may read a copy of my reference on request to the Senior Secretary.

This procedure must not preclude the subject expressing dissatisfaction to the writer. If this is not accepted the author can explain why, in their honest opinion, the complaint is unjustified. On the other hand it will occasionally happen that even the most conscientious writer of a reference is persuaded that it was not as fair as it might have been and the next reference can be improved. But it is nevertheless still, in general, best not to show the reference *before* it is sent.

This system is used only for major references, that is for full-time jobs. Often a colleague will be making a series of applications and several requests for references will come within a period of a few days. Virtually identical references can then be used, with the subject, of course, being told of the intention to do this. Where there is a reference on file that is only a few months old, I usually send a note to the subject saying I am intending to use it as it stands and asking whether there are any recent achievements they would suggest as additions.

Student references

Our system for major references on students is based on the same principles. Higher education references, for example, are monitored by the head of careers and co-ordinated by the tutor. The head of careers compiles a list of all students who intend to apply for college, polytechnic or university, using information from the students themselves, tutors, subject heads and heads of faculty. For each student, she sends subject comment forms to all who teach the student. These are returned to her, and she does any chasing necessary. Each set, when complete, is passed to the tutor who compiles the first draft of the reference.[2] Subject teachers and tutors are required to make the student aware of the general tenor of their comments, and especially of any note of reservation.

The draft reference is sent to the head or deputy head of faculty, who will usually have a discussion with the student before approving a final version. The student is informed by a memo when the reference is sent, and a copy is added to their file, and may be seen on request. So far, the number asking to see part or all of a file has been small, and have been dealt with personally. If the number increases in the future it will be no problem to let other senior staff deal with them.

Files

Files might seem an easy matter: file only essential factual information obtained with the subject's consent or which the subject knows about; allow staff and students unrestricted access to their own files; pass on information to third parties only with the subject's permission, and only pass on the minimum needed in the subject's interest. Practice is somewhat harder.

For a start, filing only factual information clearly will not do: a copy of the last reference must be kept, and that is partly opinion. And what about a report on a student sent by the social services department, or on a staff member by a doctor? To file and allow access would breach confidence with the sender; not to file it might lead to vital information being unavailable when needed to help the subject. Early in my second school headship a fifth-former died from a drug overdose. He was in his first few weeks at the school and had taken overdoses before. But his previous school had not liked to put this on file, relying instead on memory. They passed on the file but omitted to tell us of the overdoses. Had they done so, his head of house, a most caring and sensitive teacher, might have sought help from the psychological service when the boy showed signs of depression; and he might not have died.

The filing of potentially important information might also be inhibited by allowing unrestricted access to one's own file. What should the principal do when a doctor phones up to say that a member of staff, a patient of his, has a fatal illness which will allow him to work for a year or two more, and about which the doctor has not been completely honest with his patient? The principal is being told, the doctor says, because his patient's life will be prolonged if he is subject to the least possible stress. And the patient has not been told because to do so would cause him stress. The principal knows that he is, indeed, someone who might be put under pressure because there is some concern about his teaching.

Or another doctor who tells the principal that a student is under pressure because he is having a sexual relationship with his own mother, and he feels the principal must know so that he can watch carefully for any signs of suicidal depression. Because this might also be triggered by the student finding out the principal knows, it is essential to conceal this information from him or her. And from his parents, especially his father who is ignorant of what is going on when he is away. Not to file such information would be wrong. Any of us might be unexpectedly removed from the scene at any moment – the proverbial bus – and we have a duty to ensure that the welfare of those for whom we have a responsibility does not suffer as a consequence. So it must be filed, not in the ordinary file, but in a special one with access only via the principal or acting principal.

In general, the subject should know of the existence of all files on them, including those to which access is denied. However, there are very rare occasions when it must be right to lie in the interests of the subject or of someone else. The two examples I give, both drawn from personal experience some years ago, are cases where I would have lied. I filed the information separately and would have denied even the existence of the files if necessary. However, these are the only occasions when I have done this in some fifteen years of school and college headship.

Rather more frequently it is necessary to form a second file on someone with restricted access to third parties, but not to the subject. Students' files need to be available to tutors, but sometimes there is information that needs to be kept which the tutor should not know. For example, the student who tells of her abortion on condition that her tutor is not told, or who one learns has been convicted in the courts and, again, the tutor does not know.

Restricted–access files are called X files at Halesowen, and the existence of an X file is indicated by an X on the ordinary file. Some relatively innocuous information in the ordinary file may have to be kept from the student. Our partner schools supply us, at our request, with references before students come to us. These are very useful in initial placement, and we need to keep them for some time after that in case course problems arise and a change of course has to be considered. We would have no objection at all to the student seeing their school reference, but some of the schools would. The problem was discussed with the students' union and the schools/college liaison committee, and we have agreed that school references would not be shown to the student but that they will be retained only for as long as they might be useful and never for more than a year.

There is an exception to what has been said about files. The confidential counsellors[3] must keep records. But no one must see what is put on them except in the event of the counsellor who wrote it being removed from the scene and it being essential for the well-being of those being counselled that someone else take over. The counsellors' files must *not* form part of the official files of the college, and it is both legitimate and essential to conceal that they even exist. But exist they must, for the reason given.

Should parents or guardians be allowed to see the file on their son or daughter, without their permission? Obviously not if the son or daughter is over eighteen. But what if they are under eighteen? From the point of view of the student and their relationship with the college, the answer must be no. But the legal rights of the parent are ill-defined; and the parent might succeed by appealing to the local authority, who legally own the file. But they have no say over what is put in it, so it would seem to be legal to remove all potentially offensive matter and put it somewhere technically not the file.

As with references, and for the same reasons, anyone seeing their own file should not be allowed to take it away or copy it. They should, however, be allowed to challenge anything in it and ask for it to be removed or altered. If agreement cannot be reached they should have the right to have a comment of their own attached to the matter to which they object.

On the question of to whom material on file would be passed, the guiding principle is the interests of the person on whom the file is kept, for the purpose of having a file in the first place is, or should be, to promote the interest and welfare of its subject. That means giving factual information or a reference to those properly entitled to it. No third party should have unrestricted access to the file. The only exception would be '*force majeure*' – police with a search warrant, for example.

The Halesowen College handbook section on files and references is as follows:

Files and References

(a) STUDENTS
    (i) *Contents of Ordinary Files*
        A confidential file is kept on each student.
        The file contains:

Factual information passed on by the previous school
Factual information supplied by the student or her/his parents or guardians
Copies of correspondence relating to the student
Factual records of any matters for concern
Internal memoranda on the student that are of lasting importance
Copies of reports on progress
Copies of references on the student.

(ii) *X Files*

Any delicate or highly confidential material that needs to be kept is put in a special file called an X file. The existence of an X file is indicated by an X on the ordinary file.

(iii) *Security of Files*

Each ordinary file is kept in a locked filing cabinet by a designated senior member of staff. Access is allowed only to members of staff who are properly concerned with helping the student.

X files are kept by the principal and access is only via the principal or a vice principal.

(iv) *Disclosure to Third Parties*

A file would not be shown to any third party, except under circumstances such as a police search warrant or a court order, and, apart from a reference, only factual information would be revealed to anyone else.

(v) *Access to One's Own File*

Students may ask to see the contents of their own files, and will be welcome to read everything in the ordinary file that has been put there by the college. But we are not at liberty to show material that has been supplied from outside the college if it was given on the understanding that it would not be shown to the student, except with the permission of the person who supplied it. References supplied by schools or others are kept only for as long as they are relevant and never for more than a year.

Information on X files would also sometimes not be shown; it depends on what it is. But a student would always be told whether there is matter that is not being shown.

The student would not be allowed to make a copy of what is in a file, only to read it.

(vi) *Challenging the Contents of One's File*

If a student wishes to challenge anything in the file, s/he is welcome to do so, and it will either be amended, or if agreement cannot be reached, the student may have any comment s/he chooses attached to an item in the file.

(vii) *Former Students*

When a student leaves, all irrelevant information will be removed and destroyed and only essential factual information retained. Any former student may have access to her/his file on the same terms as above.

(viii) *Computer Files*

The college is in the process of computerizing part of the files. Information held on a computer will be treated as if it were in a paper file, its existence recorded and access allowed on the same terms.

(ix) *References*

The first draft of a student reference is completed by the tutor after receiving information and comments from subject teachers. The draft is checked and amended as necessary by the head or deputy head of faculty and then sent for typing and dispatch in the name of the principal. The student is informed when the reference is sent. The student would normally be made aware of the general nature of a reference. A copy is put in the student's file which may be seen on request as explained above.

(b) STAFF

There is a similar system, with similar rights of access, for staff files. Details are given in the staff guide.

There are two main differences. Staff are informed when a reference on them has been sent, and are able to read a copy on application to the senior secretary, who does *not* inform anyone when this happens.

The chief education officer also keeps a file, recording information for salary purposes and copies of LEA references supplied, on members of staff to which, at the time of writing, access is not allowed.

A system along the lines outlined above ought to be imposed on schools and colleges, not least because this is an area where not only secrecy but also sloppiness needs to be ended. The way some schools and colleges keep files is little short of a disgrace. And one thing allowing access to files does is to draw attention to how they are kept. There must, of course, be a defined system of security and of access controlled by designated people. Of course; yet this is far from always the case.

It is surprising that local authorities generally do not have detailed rules on school and college files.

Openness and complaints

Openness clearly has major implications for all aspects of the college, especially management and communications. The attitude must be to welcome complaints; to encourage them even, for it is only by finding defects in an organization that one can hope to improve it. One could argue that the main task of the principal is to find faults; and that criticism must therefore be positively welcomed. If the criticism is unjustified one has the chance to correct the complainant; if it is justified, to take action to correct the fault in the organization or apologize for the shortcoming. It is certainly a mistake to think that by discouraging complaints one suppresses criticism. All one does is to cut oneself off from the opportunity of doing anything about it.

Incidentally, I have never understood welcoming only constructive criticism. If someone points out a failing in the college organization, why on earth should I expect them also to be able to suggest how to put it right! That is my job; I should simply be grateful for having the failing drawn to my attention.

Recognizing the right to complain is surely an essential feature of democracy, removing it being almost a matter of course for tyrants and dictators. So encouraging college members to complain is beneficial to the college and is also, or ought to be, encouraging the exercise of a basic democratic right. Learning how to complain is an important part of the college's task in preparing its students for responsible citizenship.

Are sixteen-year-old students really to be encouraged to complain about members of staff? Why not? It would certainly be fatuous to tell them they can complain about anything except members of staff – presumably on the grounds that teachers are either perfect already or beyond redemption! It is, of course, a tricky and delicate matter, and careful guidance needs to be given both to students and staff. The code must be the same for students and staff, and must contain five essential elements: first, if at all possible, raise the matter with the person complained about; second, give them reasonable time to respond to the complaint; third, if that fails go to the person's immediate superior – not straight to the top – and tell the person that you are doing so; fourth, recognize there are likely to be many factors of which you are ignorant. And, most important of all, do accept that you might have made a mistake yourself.

When we were planning the tertiary college at Halesowen there were some misgivings among staff about including in the student handbook a section encouraging students to complain and telling them how to go about it. My original wording was watered down a bit and the section tucked away at the end of the handbook. Four years later the student handbook was replaced by the handbook, aimed equally at staff and students, and the section entitled "How to Complain" strengthened and put near the front. No member of staff raised any objection to this.

The section is as follows:

General
No organization is perfect; and it is only by listening to criticisms or suggestions that those who run an organization can hope to improve it. Furthermore, everyone has a fundamental right in a democracy to express their views, provided only that the equal rights of others are respected.

Any college member, therefore, has the right to complain or raise a feeling of injustice or of dissatisfaction with any aspect of college organization.

Students complaining
When raising a matter a student may choose to be accompanied by a friend, who may be an officer of the students' union.

In any organization one should avoid going over the head of an immediate superior before giving that person every opportunity to deal with the matter to one's satisfaction. So avoid, for example, going straight to a vice principal about a dissatisfaction involving a subject-teacher. Be quite open with the teacher and give her/him every opportunity to solve the problem. If you still feel dissatisfied and wish to raise the matter with someone else, tell the teacher what you are going to do, if at all possible.

It is always a good idea to get advice on how to proceed in matters like this. You could go to the students' union, the student liaison officer, a counsellor, your tutor or a senior member of staff.

In all this, do be polite and restrained; and do recognize that you might be wrong. We all make mistakes sometimes!

The principal will often be in the position of being able to strengthen or weaken the complaints procedure. If one or more students come to complain about a teacher it is tempting to hear them and attempt to solve the matter. This must be resisted. Instead, they should be advised on how to proceed. It is essential that if at all possible complaints reach the top only after the laid down procedure has been followed.

This is another example of where the principal must be seen to be bound by the same rules as the college members. It may be frustrating in a particular case; but it undoubtedly pays dividends in the longer term.

Notes

1. In August 1987 the House of Lords prohibited any newspaper in England (but not in Scotland) from quoting from or commenting on former-MI5 agent Peter Wright's book *Spycatcher*. As a result of the government's (or rather, one suspects, Mrs Thatcher's) stupidity *Spycatcher* became a bestseller, Mr Wright a rich man, and British justice an international laughing stock.
2. For notes to tutors on writing references, see Chapter 9, p. 154.
3. See Chapter 6, p. 95.

CHAPTER 8

Student involvement and the students' union

'The only thing necessary for the triumph of evil is for good men to do nothing', said Edmund Burke nearly 200 years ago. His dictum is true of nothing more than of democracy itself. There can be few objectives more important for the sixteen-plus college than educating for responsible participation in an open, multi-cultural and multi-ethnic, representative democracy. If we do not, we may not have one for much longer. No part of the college can be untouched by this. We must encourage the raising of controversial and political issues in the classroom and outside, subject to a maintenance of balance and an avoidance of indoctrination.[1] And we must clearly ensure that the college has structures and practices that exemplify and give experience of those that are essential for the sort of society for which we are preparing our students.

Unless the principal is able to abdicate his or her legal responsibilities, the college cannot itself actually *be* a democracy. But there can and should be strong democratic scrutiny of, and influence on, the running of the institution. Part of this is external, through the governors and the local education authority; part internal through whatever mechanisms for consultation and participation are prescribed or determined. Colleges under FE Regulations will usually have laid down, by their instrument and articles of government, a students' union as well as an academic board and, of course, a board of governors. And it will usually be specified that there are to be student representatives on the academic board and on the board of governors, and that there must be an approved constitution for the students' union and approved disciplinary procedures for students. Sixth-form colleges, like schools, do not have academic boards, students' unions or a specified obligation to formulate disciplinary procedures; but this is no reason for their not involving students in the college and they should set up machinery to achieve this. Many do.

While the duty of any college to educate for responsible citizenship in a representative democracy is more than a sufficient reason for involving students in the running of the institution, to do so is also an inescapable consequence of aiming to give all students a genuine feeling that the college is in a real sense "theirs". It is also, incidentally, likely to make a positive contribution to better management and to general harmony, although on particular occasions it may well make life much harder for senior management staff, especially the principal. But student involvement must be properly planned and organized to ensure that the intentions are indeed realized. There are many pitfalls.

Consultation

The first essential of consultation or delegation is honesty. Whatever the committee might be, its members and those whom they represent must know what their powers are. If the principal retains the right to overrule, then let this be made absolutely explicit. If a body is only advising it must be aware of this or there will be great indignation on the first occasion when it makes what it believes to be a binding decision only to have it overruled. In fact, there is no reason why a purely advisory body should feel weak: if the quality of its advice is good, it will almost invariably be taken, at least by any sensible management.

The second essential is that representatives should not become detached from those they represent. This is not easy to achieve with student representatives; and virtually impossible with parent ones – witness the one or two parents on a governing body purporting to speak for perhaps two thousand other parents. We certainly did not get all this right straightaway at Halesowen College, and in so far as we are correct in thinking we have learnt from some of our mistakes, it is worthwhile describing the evolution of our practice.

On student representation, unions and involvement, the easier questions are to do with powers, constitutions, and election procedures. The harder ones are: how to ensure that student representatives really do represent the views of students; how to make sure that students' union business is conducted efficiently and that there is proper financial control, without unduly circumscribing their independence, and without putting an undue burden on a small number of student officers.

Student governors and the government

There are those who think the question of what powers students should have to be one of extreme difficulty. Sir Keith Joseph certainly did when, on his last day as Secretary of State for Education and Science in 1986, he received a delegation of governors, including students, from Halesowen College arguing against the clause in his Education Bill that would have prohibited student governors under the age of eighteen.

When the College opened in 1982 the Dudley Education Authority had included its usual clause in the instrument of government – the document defining membership and procedures of the governing body – restricting student governors to being over the age of eighteen. I interpreted this as applying to the date of the first governor's meeting attended rather than the date of election, but nevertheless only a small minority of our full-time students were old enough to stand for election. As student involvement in the college developed this seemed increasingly wrong, and two years later the Dudley legal department was persuaded that there was, in fact, no legal impediment to student governors being under the age of eighteen. Governors promptly recommended the removal of the age limit, increasing the number of student governors to two at the same time, and this was approved by the authority.

After six months in which there were two excellent student governors, one under the age of eighteen, I was dismayed to discover that the government intended to make the law clear, but by categorically prohibiting any governor from being under the age of eighteen at the date of election. This would have made the situation worse than it was before the Dudley Authority removed the age limit. Clause 47 of the Education Bill (that is, a proposal for legislation) published in February 1986 read, in part, 'No person shall be qualified for membership of the governing body ... unless he is aged eighteen or over at the date of his election or appointment'. With the support of the staff and the students' union, I submitted the following paper to the governor's meeting in March 1986

It was only last September that the age limit for student governors in this college was reduced to sixteen, and their number increased from one to two. There was unanimous support from the college and its governors for these changes, and everyone, I am sure, would agree that student representation has been wholly beneficial since September.

Having student governors who are representative of the majority of students has increased the value of their contributions at governors' meetings. More importantly, allowing all students to stand for election to the governing body has symbolized our intention to treat our students as responsible young adults, and there can be no doubt that the overwhelming majority of students do respond by being responsible. The excellence of staff-student relationships and the almost total lack of vandalism or even graffiti are evidence of that.

At the beginning of the year, when elections are held, only a very small proportion of our full-time students are eighteen. That is why we all argued for the age limit to be reduced to sixteen. It is sometimes said that student representatives tend to be extremists. The chance of that is greatly increased if the majority of full-time students are ruled ineligible.

It can also be objected that only adults can assume the legal obligations and liabilities that might attach to decisions of the governing body. But in fact governors hardly do anything that has such legal consequences. And when they do it is a perfectly simple matter to debar the under-eighteens from voting. This is already done for such matters as staff appointments.

The spirit of cooperation and responsibility which characterizes this college helps our students to develop qualities that are not only beneficial to them but also the very ones that are desperately needed in society generally.

Reverting to an age bar of eighteen for student governors would, therefore, be a grave mistake and I ask the Governing Body to act to try and persuade the government to drop this proposal. Possible action could include a) passing an appropriate resolution, b) seeking a meeting with a minister of a deputation from the governing body.

Governors unanimously supported the paper and decided to seek a meeting with the Secretary of State for Education and Science. To our surprise, and pleasure, he agreed to meet us, and a party made up of the chair and shadow chair of governors, two student governors and the vice-chair of the students' union, an education officer and myself met Sir Keith Joseph in the House of Commons in May 1986.

In the course of a meeting lasting nearly an hour, he several times expressed the view that student governors would try to use their powers to make life easy for students, and he clearly was unhappy about students having a say in the running of the college. At the end he admitted to being 'More impressed with your arguments than I had expected to be'.

I followed this up with a letter to Sir Keith's successor, Kenneth Baker; and his deputy, Chris Patten, wrote to me in August saying that the government had been persuaded by our arguments and would seek to amend its own bill when it next came before parliament in October. They were as good as their word, and the bill became law as the Education (No 2) Act 1986 with Clause 47 of the bill replaced by Clause 61 which is identical except that the final line is changed to read, 'unless he is a student of the institution or is aged eighteen or over at the date of his election or appointment'. One has to read it twice to see that it does indeed remove the age limit for student governors!

Somewhat anomalously, this change was not made for colleges under schools regulations, and indeed the act does not allow for schools with sixth forms, or for sixth-form colleges, to have student governors at all.

All this was very pleasing not only for the outcome, but also for the demonstration it gave of how peaceful and reasoned lobbying can succeed – a lesson that was not lost on the students involved and which was pointed out to all the college later.

The students' union and student representation

The powers given to the students' union should be: to be consulted and advised on all matters to do with the running of the college and to determine the spending of their own money subject only to its being within their constitution and to proper financial procedures. To restrict the involvement of students to such matters as the rules for the use of the common rooms, running discos and advising on cafeteria menus is demeaningly patronizing and totally inconsistent with the sort of aims advocated in the previous chapter.

Why on earth should seventeen- and eighteen-year-olds *not* advise on the organization of the timetable, on times of day and length of classes, on effectiveness of teaching? They certainly are affected by all of these, and their views, especially on the last, should be given great weight. And why not on appointment of staff and other staffing matters, subject only to the proviso that the rights of staff must be safeguarded? How far one can go will depend on the staff themselves, and on governors and education officers; and it would probably be unwise to set up a college with such a total involvement of students from the outset. Rather, involvement can be increased over the years as confidence in it increases. And that will, to a considerable extent, depend on the effectiveness of student organization, a much more difficult question.

Under FE Regulations, college articles of government will require both that there be a students' union and that its constitution be submitted to governors for approval. It is not uncommon in FE colleges, and even tertiary colleges, for this to be something of a dead letter. This is a mistake. The requirement to formulate a students' union constitution is a splendid opportunity to get students involved in organizing themselves, as well as of pointing out to staff and governors the purpose and the value of active student participation. Indeed, there is a lot to be said for making this a continuing debate, with amended constitutions being put before governors every year or two as each generation of students modifies and improves the procedures inherited from the previous generation. It is easy for the staff to forget the extent to which students are transient. To have consulted students four years ago may satisfy us, but is not likely to impress the students, virtually none of whom were in the college then. They can hardly be expected to feel it is 'their' college if constitutions and procedures established before they came are considered immutable.

Having a union at all can provoke opposition. At Halesowen there was quite a bit from parents who took a dim view of trade unions in general and feared we would be inculcating the students with the sort of disruptive activity which has certainly occurred in Britain and which, thanks to our irresponsible tabloid press, they saw as being an inevitable concomitant of trade unionism. The college must not yield to this reaction, but instead must proclaim that trade unions are fundamental to a democracy and the college therefore has a duty to set up a students' union that will be a model of what a trade union can be. The belief that any union must be a disruptive force can be disproved by what actually happens – with careful planning and a bit of luck! But there are other objections.

Is the students' union not a closed shop? In the sense that all students are automatically members, it is. But so long as there is no levy on students paid directly to the union it can be maintained that it is grant-funded by the local authority on the basis of the total number of students in the college, so there is no compulsory union fee levied on students.

Many parents will also feel that it would be wrong for sixteen-year-olds to be forced into political activity by, say, the students' union affiliating to the Labour Party or the Campaign for Nuclear Disarmament, or even the National Union of Students (NUS). One can see their point. It is one thing for their sixteen-year-old son or daughter to be obliged to be a member of an organization that aims to exemplify a model trade union; it is quite another to be associated with particular political views and campaigns. Nevertheless affiliating to the NUS has definite benefit; it gives good advice on organization and administration as well as running excellent short training courses for union officers.

The Halesowen Student's Union Constitution is worded to allow NUS affiliation but to prevent the union from being politicized. It has the following statement of aims:

- To involve all members of the union in democratic participation in decision making in the college.
- To advance the general education of its members.
- To aid the development of the corporate life of the college.
- To maintain communication among the student members of the college; and to advise and assist individual students in eduational, welfare and disciplinary matters.
- To represent the views of the student body on such college bodies as may be agreed by the governors.
- To act as a channel for discussion between students and the principal.
- To promote and coordinate cultural and social activities in the college.
- To advise individual members in matters affecting their welfare and to promote the welfare of the student body as a whole.
- To encourage participation in athletic, recreational and community activities.
- To promote and foster good relations between the college and the community and between the college and other educational institutions.

While the constitution does not specifically preclude the union from political campaigning, it does so implicitly in that anything not covered by the aim is unconstitutional, and the interpretation of the constitution is not in the hands of the union. Section 19 of the constitution reads:

> The president, in consultation with the council and the student liaison officer, shall be responsible for ensuring that the union functions as specified in this constitution. The governors are the final arbiters on constitutional matters and there is a general right of appeal to them on the constitution. The principal shall act as an immediate arbiter on the constitution, subject to subsequent ratification by governors, to whom any decision taken by him on the interpretation of this constitution shall be reported.

At first I believed that the union should be totally non-political. If a group of students wanted to form a college branch of a political party, the union would offer help regardless of whether the officers were supporters or opponents, provided only that the aims of the party were compatible with those of the college. This remains my position, but I have changed my mind on a second point, namely whether the union should be able to engage in political activity affecting the college.

During teacher industrial action in 1986 it struck me as anomalous that while staff unions were required by law to ballot their members before taking action, there was no similar requirement for the students' union. So after discussion with the student liaison officer and the union officers, I inserted a new clause in the constitution, which was approved by governors in June 1987. It reads as follows:

STUDENT PROTEST ACTION

Students may organize action likely to cause disruption of the college, including encouraging any student to be absent from a scheduled timetable commitment, only through the students' union, and for such action to be constitutional *all* the following conditions must have been met:

(1) The proposed action must be precisely defined in a proposal.
(2) A resolution for a secret referendum of the union on this proposal must be put before a properly convened meeting of the full council of the union.
(3) This resolution must be passed by a two-thirds majority of those present.

(4) The secret referendum of the entire membership must be carried out under the procedures of this constitution, with the count conducted in the presence of a union officer and the student liaison officer or assistant principal in charge of student affairs.

(5) The wording of the proposal that is the subject of the referendum must state only the action that is proposed. It must not be worded in a way that suggests how members should vote, and must be in a form that requires the answer to be Yes or No.

(6) A majority of the total membership of the union must vote Yes.

Admirably, the student officers in 1985 felt very strongly that racism should be grounds for expelling a student from the union. But what is racism, and who determines that someone is guilty of it? After much debate, the following sentence was included in the constitution: 'Overt membership of or support for any organization that is racist, or the continued assertion of racist views, shall be deemed incompatible with membership of the union.' Taken in conjunction with Section 19, quoted earlier, this has enabled the union to proclaim its commitment to racial equality without there being any danger of arbitrary exercise of power by the union officers.

As in everything else, the attitudes of teaching staff are of great significance. If every tutor and subject teacher manifestly views the union, and student involvement in it, as important, this will have a considerable effect right across the college; but if the attitude is lukewarm in some sections, this will probably be reflected by student apathy in those sections.

Student representation must obviously not be fragmented, and all student representatives on the board of governors and on academic board need to be automatic members of the students' union committee even if elected separately. Fragmentation can also occur – it did with us – if separate bodies such as a rag committee exist alongside the union. The answer may be to make the rag committee a separately elected sub-committee of the union committee with the president of the union *ex officio* on the sub-committee.

General meetings of students

Having achieved a single committee representing all students, it must be decided what they will do, how they will be helped and how they will keep in touch with the mass of students they represent. One means, at Halesowen, are the students' meetings held at the beginning of each term.[2] With over 1,200 full-time students and no large hall, around ten meetings are necessary to cover all students. Despite the monotony for me, and those who accompany me, we stick to the same format and content for each meeting. After a brief talk from me on what is happening in the college – building works, staff shortages or changes and so on – a few words are said by the student liaison officer, the president of the students' union and the confidential counsellors. They all say something of their role, and we all speak from the shared assumption of its being 'our' college. There is no doubt that students value these meetings at the beginning of each term. The original request for them came from students, and when in April 1987 I suggested that it was not worth the disruption to hold student meetings at the beginning of the summer term, the students' union consulted every tutor group through the student council members and reported an overwhelming vote in favour of meetings. They said they valued the principal taking the trouble to address them and felt the meetings reaffirmed the personal touch that was a hallmark of our college.

Once a year the annual general meetings of the students' union have to be held; there have to be several of these because we cannot get all students who want to attend into our largest space. They give the union officers, advised by the liaison officer, a chance to learn about conducting a large meeting. So far these meetings have gone impressively well and have been very well-organized, with tannoys, a platform, marshalls, voting stewards, printed notices and agendas for everyone. Apart from their immediate purpose, they are a valuable educational experience for students.

Students' union welcoming new students

Before and at the beginning of the new college year, last year's officers, many of whom will have left and be waiting to go to university or polytechnic, can play a most important part in ensuring that the incoming students build on what has already been achieved. It was such students who suggested, a few years ago, that a letter should be sent from the outgoing union executives to new students, welcoming them to the college and the union, and this has been done every year since, enclosing it with the final batch of information posted in August.

Student elections

At Halesowen, elections for the students' union officers and for student representatives on the board of governors and academic board are held during the first few weeks of the autumn term. These elections are a major item in the meeting for students at the start of each college year. Last year's officers come to these also and new students especially are impressed by what they have to say about the union and the part it plays in the college. As a consequence, the elections soon attract great interest. A week is allowed for nominations, and the union then organizes one or more meetings. Students are allowed to miss classes, if necessary, to attend one meeting, at which each of the candidates is introduced and invited to speak briefly.

The procedure for the elections, as laid down in the students' union constitution, is widely circulated and followed rigorously. The relevant sections of the constitution are:

5. (4) The officers shall be elected at the beginning of the academic year to serve for the period until the elections for the following year.

(5) Any member of the students' union may be nominated for offices of the union. Nominations shall be proposed, seconded and countersigned by the nominee to indicate willingness to stand. Nominations shall be delivered by hand to the returning officer.

(6) A period of at least one week shall be allowed for nominations.

(7) When the period for nominations has elapsed one or more general meetings of the students' union shall be held at which the candidates will be introduced and given an opportunity to address the meeting.

(8) The election shall be carried out by secret ballot, extending over a period of one week, enabling all registered students of the college to cast their vote.

(9) The simple majority system of voting shall be employed to determine the result of the election.

The student liaison officer is the returning officer, and the count is carried out as in a parliamentary election, with candidates watching and consulted on any dubious ballot forms.

Union meetings

At Halesowen we have three upward channels of communication.[3] One is the students' union executive. It comprises the five union officers (president, vice-president, secretary, treasurer and press officer), the two student governors and the three academic board representatives. They meet the principal once a fortnight and can raise any matter. They are also consulted on a wide range of issues, and are kept informed of what is going on by being sent minutes of other meetings, including those of the senior college management team, and copies of relevant letters.

Minutes are issued after each meeting. Some years I do them, because it is easy for me to dictate the minutes into a dictaphone immediately after the meeting and get them typed up and distributed without delay. Anything the students wanted to challenge would be corrected at the next meeting. In other years the students prefer to do the minutes themselves, and this has the advantage of giving experience to some in the art of minute-taking.

Copies of these minutes, and of the other two upward channels of communication, automatically go to the next weekly meeting of the management team, and students can see that the matters they raise are treated seriously. Copies also go to the students' union council.

The council is a device we introduced to bridge the gap between the Executive and the rest of the students. To prevent it being too large, tutor groups are paired to form constituencies of about thirty students, each with one elected council member. The council meets monthly with the union executive, and meetings are properly advertised, structured and minuted.

Staff–student liaison officer

Clearly the union will need staff help; and on financial matters especially there must be ultimate staff control. Like other colleges, we have a teacher who is given time to act as staff–student liaison officer. This is a job requiring a rare combination of talents: acceptability to both staff and students, an appreciation of college policy at a high level and a sensitivity to young people, considerable organizing ability yet a preparedness not to interfere unless absolutely essential. At first we thought we must have a senior member of staff – an assistant principal – but we came to see that seniority is an impediment rather than an advantage. We now recruit from junior staff, but a problem is that if they have the qualities needed they are not likely to remain junior for long.

The staff–student liaison officer, despite being on a junior salary scale, is one of the most important people in the college. Our present liaison officer walks around and talks to groups of students from all parts of the college – it is amazing how many students claim to know him. He is trusted absolutely by the Union officers, who do not believe for one moment that he is any sort of staff spy in their midst, but that on the contrary he is someone who is an invariable source of friendly help and advice.

Nevertheless, at times his position can become difficult and even, conceivably, impossible. Disputes between principal and students can arise. One reached the point of the union being about to organize a sit-in of my office because they felt I was brushing aside a legitimate objection to a proposal to increase the length of classes from one to one-and-a-half-hours. The staff–student liaison officer sympathized with their case but felt they had not exhausted consultation and ought to hold back. He was right; but that did not make his position any easier during two fraught days, throughout which he had to keep on speaking terms with both the principal and the students' union president without losing the confidence of either. Fortunately both sides came to see they were partly wrong. The union called off the sit-in; I apologized for not taking sufficient note of their points, and a joint meeting of students' union executive and the entire management team cleared the air and led to agreement. Through their council, and the announcements circulated, most students were able to follow this dispute, and its outcome did much to reassure them that the college really is a partnership between all of us.

But the point, in this context, is that had there not been such an outcome, the staff–student liaison officer would have been in an impossible position, and would have had to choose between the principal and the union. I am inclined to think the liaison officer must choose the union in such a situation, on the grounds that as there will probably still be a principal afterwards, one might as well ensure that there is also a staff–student liaison officer. And if the liaison officer thinks the union is in the wrong, s/he should still stay in contact with the union, possibly without expressing an opinion at all to the principal, while remaining publicly agnostic.

It must be accepted that disputes between principal and union might occur which would do damage to relationships, and that they might be set back months. One cannot control free elections – by definition – and to nominate student officers would defeat the main purpose of having them. Therefore one must accept the possibility of the wrong people being elected and of otherwise avoidable disputes poisoning the atmosphere. Provided all the other aspects of staff–student relationships are satisfactory, the transient nature of the student population means that things will probably be different with the next student intake. We had one such dispute at Halesowen in our first year. While very upsetting at the time, six months later it was as if it had never happened.

The liaison officer also had a vital role with his or her own colleagues. Not all staff will be equally committed to making the union effective; not all will be equally punctilious in seeing their own tutor group is properly informed about and represented on the council; not all will equally strongly urge students to participate, to stand for election and to vote; not all will be equally willing to release students for union duties. The liaison officer needs to be very effective at cajoling colleagues who fail in any of these.

Union duties

Time out of class for union duties is a difficult one. If the officers do not have the time they cannot do their job properly; if they do, they might fail their examinations. One part-solution is to have an activities afternoon right across the college and allow union work as one of the designated activities.

Nevertheless, however well the timetable is organized and the union work spread, the good union will be likely to make excessive demands on some of its student officers. The student support system must be alert to this; and tutors in particular need to counsel union officers in their group regularly. And the college must be prepared to advise a student to resign a union office if the demands are greater than can be borne without damage to the student's examination and career prospects. In any case, an occasional by-election during the year is no bad thing. It can rekindle general interest in the union as well as bring fresh blood on to the committee.

In this, as in everything else, the staff of the college must balance the interests of individuals against those of the college generally. Provided this is done, a period of office in the students' union can be a most valuable experience for a seventeen- or eighteen-year-old, as well as being of great value to the rest of the college.

Notes

1. See also Chapter 5, pp. 83–84.
2. This has now been done by a regulation having the force of law, namely the Education Governing Bodies of Institutions of Further Education Regulations 1987, issued by the secretary of state in July 1987 and having effect from September 1987. Regulation number 4 prohibits governors under the age of eighteen from playing any part in any proposal:
   (a) for the expenditure of money by the governing body: or
   (b) under which the governing body, or any members of the governing body, would enter into any contract, or would incur any debt or liability (whether immediate, contingent or otherwise).
3. See Chapter 9, pp. 150–152.

PART FIVE

Evaluating administration

CHAPTER 9

Information

A central theme of this book is that every activity of the college must be imbued with the aims. How something is done is as important as what is done. This is true of the college communications system, of the parts and of the whole.

Language and paper

A message, whether written or oral, creates an impression by its wording, style and manner that is additional to its factual content. Sloppy format or pompous wording has an effect regardless of the information conveyed. But, of course, information will not be conveyed at all unless the presentation and style are sufficiently attractive to gain and keep the attention of the reader, and the wording sufficiently clear for the content to be readily and unambiguously understood.

If bulletins, notices and memos consist of large numbers of identically coloured and laid out pieces of paper full of turgid officialese, they are hardly likely to grab the reader and communications will be poor. Were it not for the fact that so many organizations, including many government departments and local education authorities, do fail to communicate effectively, it would seem superfluous to state the elementary principle of communication: relevant content in language geared to the reader and an attractive and distinctive presentation. The acres of gobbledegook churned out daily by local and national government officials are enough to make Sir Ernest Gowers[1] turn in his grave. Their anonymous authors may never split an infinitive or finish a sentence with a preposition, but they all too often use ten polysyllables to obscure where fewer and shorter words would clarify.

It is essential that senior staff should seek to conform to these injunctions in all their own memos and letters. Some will be better at this than others, but all must be equal in the importance they attach to clarity of language. Each must be prepared to learn from others, and to receive, and *give* criticism. Professional educators tend to shy away from these, especially the last, as if to suggest that a colleagues' English could be improved is somehow beyond the limits allowed by good manners. This is nonsense. None of us is perfect; and if a task is important, it is foolish not to give oneself the opportunity of learning how to do it better and one should welcome criticism and, in turn, see it as a duty to give criticism when we can. As principal, I skim copies of every official college letter or memo, and do not hesitate to criticize style and wording when I feel able to do so helpfully. But I also make it clear that any college member has a reciprocal duty to criticize my communications. Not infrequently, they do; and I usually agree with their points and am always grateful for their making them.

So use a simple, direct style, have a clear layout and make different publications readily distinguishable. Paper comes in many different colours – a fact that seems to have escaped the faceless clerks. Any organization should design a colour-coding scheme so that lists of paper can be more easily distinguished by their colours. It's hard luck on the colour-blind, but most are not and will find a colour-coding system helpful. It all adds to the impression that communicating is taken seriously. And nothing should be anonymous or undated – from whom the message came, and when, is of immediate interest to the reader and essential for accurate filing.

Channels of communication

What communication channels are set up is as important as whether they are efficient. If the official system has a consultative committee for teaching staff but not support staff, what does that say to the support staff about the importance attached to their views? Or to the students about the importance attached to the students' union if there is no official channel linking the officers with those they represent?

The official system must, therefore, be comprehensive, and it needs to be the common property of all. Not only does this encourage unity and the feeling that it is 'our' college, but it will also tend to make the system work better as everyone has a vested interest in it.

Lacking a morning assembly and having large numbers of part-time students, the tertiary college must perforce have longer lines of communication than a school and therefore rely more on intermediaries. Almost certainly, information will be sent to students only via tutors, and probably to parents via tutors and students.

Those at the end of the line will be reached with any degree of certainty only if the intermediaries are reliable; and their reliability will depend on the importance they attach to the task. This requires a general recognition of the importance of good communications and a general commitment to making the system work. It only needs a small number to fail to carry out their part for the system to be paralysed.

Most lines of internal communication are in one of three directions: down from the principal or senior staff to other college members; up from these college members; and sideways between different groups of college members. Up and down lines are relatively easy to set up and operate, but they must be kept separate. A committee may be very good at putting the views of those it represents but is unlikely to be anything like as effective in passing messages back to them. This is partly because it lacks the mechanism: its members can get the views of colleagues by informal conversation or asking for written comments, but will probably have no means of sending messages to them except by using another channel. But, in addition, its members, having volunteered to do a representing job, are not going to relish being asked to do the different one of acting as messengers from the top to their colleagues. So keep up and down lines separate.

This reminds one of a railway system. So does the fact that most lines are to or from the capital. Cross-country lines for communicating sideways are much harder to construct, and often the only connection is through the centre.

Regular bulletins

Almost any college will have a system of regular information bulletins, probably weekly. At Halesowen, fairly unremarkably, we have a weekly bulletin, which we call the 'Calendar of Events'. It is compiled on Thursday evening for issue to tutors on Friday afternoon. Tutors pass on the contents to full-time students at the tutor group at the beginning of the week. They are expected to draw students' attention to items of particular interest and to pin up the copy in the room used for tutor group meetings.

The events calendar is intended for staff as well as students, so copies are pinned up in staff rooms and offices as well as being given to key people, especially the caretakers. To be effective such a bulletin needs to be both brief and full of information, a balance that is not easy to strike. Ours normally runs to four sides of A4, with the first half a list of events against each day and the second general notices. Some students and part-time staff will not see the bulletin until two or three days after it is published, so it needs to cover more than a week and overlap with the previous and the next one. If the list of events is regularly incomplete, less and less notice will be taken of it, so everyone must be chivvied into reporting to the compiler any event they are organizing and a fuss made when an event is missed.

The second half of such a bulletin must not become a ragbag of assorted notices and advertisements or tutors will not be inclined to go through it properly with their groups. A small ads section detracts from the bulletin, and should be assigned to specified notice boards in the college, not the bulletin.

There is a contradiction, or at any rate a difficulty, in the aims of a tertiary college that has already been referred to in Chapter 4 and is particularly apparent when designing its communication system. On the one hand the college aims to generate a sense of community among its members, and this must imply to some extent that they are distinct from those who are not members. Yet, on the other hand, it seeks to be a community resource, part of the wider community outside the college, and to that end large numbers of people of all ages are encouraged to become part-time students, ranging from the unemployed doing fifteen or so hours a week to those on one-day-a-week job-release courses and a host of adults taking evening classes.

With part-time members, especially, what to communicate needs to be considered first, there being little point in agonizing over creating lines of communication if there is nothing to send along them. The weekly bulletin is not likely to be of much interest to fifty-year-olds attending one evening a week for one term for a welding or keep-fit class, so it is hardly worth the effort of trying to get copies to them. But from the point of view of encouraging external support for the college, it is worth giving them the chance to see bulletins and other college publications. Their attention can be drawn to the copies pinned up in the room they use, and spare copies can be put out in the coffee lounges they use.

In practice, and even unconsciously, the communications system will divide the college staff and students into two distinct groups, full- or nearly full-time members who do get all bulletins, publications and notices, and the rest who do not. The first group should be defined as widely as is possible, and should certainly include all part-time day students, both teenage and adult, with the possible exception of those who spend a very small amount of time in college, such as those on drop-in sessions for the unemployed or senior citizens. But even here, it is gratifying to discover how often they are delighted to be included.

While there are no hard and fast rules about this dichotomy, not least because no two colleges are the same, with some having several sites including far-flung annexes catering for very occasional clients, it is fundamental that everything should be done to make the full-time students aware of the part-time students, including mixing them up whenever practicable.

But I digress. The weekly bulletin – or whatever the college decides on – will be the core of the internal communications system, and everything possible needs to be done to make it effective. Failure to put items in for inclusion should be treated as a serious matter and the staff or students responsible admonished. And senior staff must set an example by using the weekly bulletin whenever possible and not issuing separate notices needlessly. Care must be taken over the presentation of the bulletin. It merits having a member of the management team responsible for its production, and the principal should proof-read every issue, not to censor but to check it is presented and written effectively and, incidentally, to indicate to all the college how important the bulletin is.

Notices

Nevertheless, many notices from senior staff will need to be issued separately, sometimes because they are of interest only to certain staff or because their matter is semi-confidential. It helps if these also are colour-coded. There will never be enough colours for all distinctions, but some are better than none, provided they are invariably adhered to. It is, therefore, essential to maintain adequate supplies of all the different colours needed. Perhaps the biggest enemy of this aspect of communications is the cluttered notice board. Notice boards need to be carefully laid out, and it is best to have several so that, for example, notices from the staff association, the examinations officer and the principal are on different boards. Notice boards on which new notices appear frequently should be divided into sections such as: 'New Today', 'Current' and 'Previous'. It is essential that notices under the first of these headings really are new each day, or the impact will be lost. So someone needs to undertake the task, and it is an important one, of moving notices across each day. To avoid the 'Previous' section getting cluttered, notices can be moved from it to a file on a table nearby after, say, a week.

Attractive notices on well set out boards are essential to ensure this channel works well. The other is that the target group actually looks at the boards daily. All college members need, therefore, to have a place – it need not be the same for everyone – to which they go daily, among other things, to read notices.

The more interesting, informative and important notices are, the more likely are people to get into the habit of reading them. And they need also to be up to date. If it is important to keep colleagues and students informed about what is going on, it is important to do so promptly. So after every meeting of general interest, a brief account of what took place needs to appear within a day or two at the most. This applies especially to meetings of governors, the academic board and management team (or whatever the senior internal committee is called). It is no good waiting until the minutes are confirmed at the next meeting. In the case of governors that could be three months later! Either unconfirmed minutes or a separate account needs to be put up straightaway. It does not matter that these will be subject to later confirmation. In this, it is better to be quick than totally accurate.

Both weekly bulletins and notices on boards need to be relatively brief and are not suitable for longer items or for communication with parents. They can therefore profitably be supplemented by an occasional newsletter of greater length. At Halesowen the principal's newsletter appears twice a term. Its introductory paragraph reads something as follows: 'Newsletters are issued two or three times a term and are intended to help keep everyone informed about what is going on. Students, especially those under eighteen, are asked to pass their copy on to their parents or guardians.' It usually runs to about eight sides of A4. Since we took to having tutors put the student's name on the top, very few have been found lying around and sample surveys of parents and guardians show that nearly all are being delivered. Although written by the principal, others, most notably the students' union and the parent governors, are always asked to contribute sections. Copies are given to governors as part of the principal's report for scheduled meetings. Copies of the last issue of the summer term are sent to prospective students in August and thereby serve the additional purpose of familiarizing incoming students and their parents with this part of the communication system.

Parents' association

When we were planning the college we intended to have a parent–teacher association and parental involvement along the lines of the best of school practice. This has not happened. Our initial efforts met with little response, and we then came to believe that parental involvement was, to a considerable degree, incompatible with the sort of student involvement we were developing. We may be wrong in this, and other colleges may be able to demonstrate that we are. Nevertheless, it does seem to us that the student involvement we have achieved depends on explicitly treating students as having responsibilities both for their own studies and for the college generally. Most do respond admirably and, therefore, to set up a school-type parents' association would, we think, be taken as implying that students are to be treated as school-type pupils. I think that the lack of response from parents to tentative moves to start a parents' association stemmed more from a recognition of this than from apathy.

So we do not have a parents' association; but parents do receive progress reports on students under the age of eighteen and are invited to parents evenings to discuss their student son or daughter's progress. They can also become involved if there is any cause for concern over work or behaviour. But here, again, we start with the assumption of students accepting personal responsibility for their own lives.

It is not that partnership with parents is unimportant; on the contrary, it is of very great importance indeed that parents should have a strong feeling that the college is working with them to help their children. But the nature of that partnership must take account of other factors, most notably the way the college treats its students.

Handbooks

Some of the information sent down from the top (or out from the centre if this model is preferred) is semi-permanent and best included in a booklet. Prospectuses should not be used for this purpose; they are for information required by applicants, not those who have actually joined. Probably most schools and colleges recognize the need for a set of standing orders for the teaching staff, usually available for consultation in one or two specified places and some will give a copy to every teacher. Some extend the staff guide to cover non-teaching staff as well, and a few sixth-form and tertiary colleges also give each full-time student a student guidebook. But I know of only one that has a handbook for all full or nearly full-time college members, whether support staff, teaching or students, admittedly supplemented by a staff guide for the support and teaching staff.

At first, at Halesowen, we had a student handbook, a copy being given to every full-time student. The first issue was written jointly by the students' union president and the principal before the new tertiary college opened, and the next three editions were improved versions based on criticisms and suggestions from staff and students. Alongside the student handbook were developed the two prospectuses, for full- and part-time courses, the staff information book and the brief guide. This last was produced to give general information about the college to potential applicants for staff posts and to the many educationalists who visit us.

After four years we amalgamated the brief guide and the student handbook, adding some of what had been in the staff information book, to produce the handbook. Extracts are given in several places elsewhere in this book. The table of contents given below indicates its scope.

Preface
The College Aims
Obligations of College Membership
How to Complain
The Students' Union
The Tutor and Faculty System
Liberal and Recreational Studies
Communications
Student Services
  (a) Careers
  (b) Confidential Counselling
  (c) Principal's Fund
  (d) First Aid and the Welfare Assistant
The Library
Visits and Excursions
Eating in College
Files and References
  (a) Students
     (i)   Contents of Ordinary Files
     (ii)   X Files
     (iii) Security of Files
     (iv) Disclosure to Third Parties
     (v)   Access to One's Own File
     (vi) Challenging the Contents of One's Own File
     (vii) Former Students
     (viii) Computer Files
     (ix) References
  (b) Staff
The Government and Management of the College
  (a) Legal Framework
  (b) Governors
  (c) Academic Board
  (d) Management Team
Staff Lists
  (a) Support Staff
  (b) Teaching Staff
Students Costs
Personal Property; Security, Loss and Insurance
Public Examinations
Rules
Vehicles and Cycles
Student Discipline System

History of the College
Times of Day
Calendar 1986/7

There are also several photographs of members of the teaching and support staff. These are put in partly to make the booklet more attractive but mainly to emphasize the personal touch in our college. The current edition has photographs of the principal, the two vice-principals, the six assistant principals, the chief administrative officer, the senior secretary, the librarian, the confidential counsellors, the careers counsellor, the college nurse, the teachers who organize liberal studies and recreational studies, the student liaison officer and the three caretakers.

Communications system

One thing that needs to be communicated is the communications system itself. This the Halesowen handbook attempts to do, and part of the section on communications reads as follows:

1. WEEKLY CALENDAR OF EVENTS
   A copy goes to every tutor late Friday afternoon. The tutor draws students' attention to important items, and the calendar is then pinned up in the tutor room. Items for inclusion – and suggestions are welcome – need to be handed in at the college reception in Block One by 9 am on Thursday.

2. PRINCIPAL'S NEWSLETTER
   Every five or six weeks copies are given to all full-time students via tutors with the aim of keeping students and their parents, and staff and governors, fully informed about what is going on in the college. Suggestions for items to be included are very welcome.

3. PROGRESS REPORTS
   (a) *Full-Time Students*
   Reports consist of single-subject comment slips, together with a tutor's comment and a student's comment slip, stapled together in a small folder. A blank slip is enclosed for parents of students under eighteen to acknowledge receipt and make any comments they wish. Reports for most students are issued halfway through the first year, at the end of the first year and again halfway through the second year.

(b) *Part-Time Students*

For part-time students sponsored by a firm or agency, single-sheet reports are sent to the agency or firm as agreed with them.

4. PARENTS' EVENINGS

At least once a year, for each group of full-time students, a parents evening is held to enable parents, accompanied by students if they wish, to have further discussion with tutors and subject teachers.

5. CAREERS EVENINGS

From time to time meetings for students and their parents are organized in conection with particular aspects of careers. For example, an evening meeting on higher education is held in June for first-year A-level students.

6. DISCUSSION EVENINGS

Occasional discussion evenings are held when parents, students and staff are invited to come and raise with the principal any college or educational matter they wish.

7. OPEN DAY

The annual Open Day is held in the Autumn Term. Its main purpose is to advertise the college to employers and prospective students. It also gives an opportunity for parents, college members, governors and education officers to see aspects of the college and its work of which they might have been unaware.

8. INDIVIDUAL MEETINGS INVOLVING STUDENTS AND PARENTS

At the request of a student, her/his parents or teachers, a special meeting about an individual student can be arranged at any time.

9. INFORMAL VISITS BY PARENTS OR FRIENDS

Parents and friends of the college are welcome to come and walk around – perhaps combining the visit with a meal in one of the training restaurants.

The handbook needs to be supplemented by a much larger and more comprehensive compendium of information, procedures and regulations for staff. At first, by staff request, we issued a copy to each member of the teaching staff and certain members of the support staff. It was in the form of an A4 ring binder so that pages could be replaced or added. At the end of each year, all these binders were collected in and reissued, with major revisions, at the beginning of the next. The system was a failure. Not all staff kept their binders up to date, and some forgot to hand them in at the end of the year, so that a large proportion of those in circulation at any given time were inaccurate. Furthermore, we never managed to get the revised version out in time for the beginning of the year.

After four years of trying, unsuccessfully, to make this system work, we changed it. The handbook is now for both staff and students, and every college member gets a copy. We also send copies to applicants for staff posts at the college.

The new staff guide is now more accurately targeted at staff. There are copies in the staff lounge, the library, and held by senior staff such as heads of faculty. Other staff were offered their own copies on request. About forty did ask for, and were given, a copy. In doing so, they accept an obligation to keep their own copy up to date. All sheets in the guide are dated, so out–of–date guides can be recognized. When replacement sheets are issued the old ones have to be returned, and this is checked so that we can be fairly sure that out–of–date sheets are not in circulation. We therefore no longer need to collect in all the guides at the end of each year.

Consultative committees

Upward communication is formalized through the consultative committees, of which there are four at Halesowen: the academic board,[2] mainly staff but including three student representatives; the students' union executive and council; and the two staff committees. In addition, the unions also serve the purpose of communicating upwards.

Academic board can be a powerful vehicle for involving all the college in major policy matters, and it will be weakened if it devotes time to matters that, in policy terms, are relatively trivial, such as car parking, litter, meal queues and so no. But these matters can be very important indeed to those who wish to raise them and to the efficient running of the college. While it is desirable, and I believe essential, for the principal and senior staff to walk around and to be accessible, it is a delusion that this is sufficient and formal systems for channelling complaints upwards must be set up. Those at Halesowen are described in the handbook as follows:

10. STUDENTS' UNION
    The principal meets the SU executive committee regularly. Minutes of meetings are circulated and also put before the next meeting of management team.

11. STAFF CONSULTATIVE BODIES
There are three. The academic board is made up of the
principal and management team, staff and student
representatives, and is a statutory body. It meets about
twice a term.

SSCC (Support Staff Consultative Committee) consists
of elected representatives of the different sections of
support staff. It meets the principal about once a month.
Minutes are circulated and also put before the next meeting
of management team.

TSCC (Teaching Staff Consultative Committee)
functions in the same way as SSCC and has two
representatives elected from each faculty.

While academic board will have its terms of reference defined by
the articles of government, staff consultative committees will not.
Any attempt to define what may be legitimately raised at these
meetings risks being interpreted as trying to stifle criticism.

Nevertheless, there need to be some limits. Individual grievances
have an element of confidentiality about them, and may develop in
ways which should not be public for the sake of the people
concerned. They should be handled by the individuals concerned,
or by their union, or by someone else acting on their behalf, and
any attempt to raise an individual grievance should be ruled out of
order at the consultative committee.

Complaints about, or sniping at, an individual are tricky; but
should be allowed unless the person under attack is relatively
junior. Middle and senior management should be thick-skinned
enough to accept they will be criticized, often unfairly, and should
recognize that it is only if a criticism is brought out into the open
that it can be rebutted if unjustified or responded to if not. And
even if one suspects malice, it is best to affect to notice none and to
respond only to the substance of what is raised. Malice derives its
satisfaction from eliciting anger or distress in the target. If none is
apparent, malicious criticism is discouraged.

Consultative committees will often raise matters that are the
proper preserve of academic board. While academic board must be
the final place to discuss such matters, and the only body to tender
advice on them, it seems ridiculous to say that no other body
should discuss them at all. Indeed, academic board discussion will
be all the better for preliminary discussion elsewhere. But, of
course, no decision must be taken prior to academic board giving
its considered advice.

considered advice.

Unlike academic board, consultative committees function best without agendas so that anyone can raise anything. But they need minutes, partly so that those they represent can see what was raised and partly so that the minutes can be passed on to the college management team and every point raised given a proper response either immediately or after further consideration.

Lateral communication

So much for upward communication. Sideways communication, between people in different parts of the college of roughly equal rank, is hard to write about or formalize without becoming excessively bureaucratic. Yet it is undoubtedly important. It cannot be formalized to any great extent, but rather comes from a recognition by everyone that it needs to be done. And that recognition is the product of several factors, the most important being a sense of unity and common purpose and the practice of senior staff demonstrating the importance attached by the college to good communications. In other words, if the aims of the college are important to all its members, and if a good system of upward and downward communications has been set up, college members are much more likely to recognize the importance of keeping other colleagues informed of what they are doing. Indeed, it is not unknown for staff to keep colleagues in the dark deliberately so that they can steal a march on them. Sideways communication is, therefore, something of a barometer. If it is good, and people are definitely trying to keep others informed, it will be because they recognize the importance of working with, not against, colleagues in other parts of the college, and this is a demonstration of unity and common purpose. Conversely, failures in sideways communications may be accidental, but may not, and senior staff should always take heed of them. They may indicate the beginning of a diminution in morale or sense of purpose.

Communications, then, are an integral part of the organization, and through the system of communications that is set up is communicated not only content but also the attitude of the principal and senior staff to other members of the college. Its importance cannot be exaggerated.

The same objectives, of clarity and candour, should inform the college's communications with the outside world. Many of these –

prospectuses, reports to governors, newsletters, and so on – will be in the name of the principal and written either by the principal or a senior colleague. As far as possible, drafts should be circulated for criticism before the final version is issued. Both accuracy and English are likely to be better as a result. And the sense of working together as a team will be incidentally enhanced. Criticism from other members of the college and parents should be invited. After all, the readers are in the best position to judge the effectiveness of a communication. All specialisms tend to develop their own jargon. While unintelligible to the outsider, jargon may be an aid to communication among the initiated. But I suspect not, and while some acronyms can be essential for brevity, they seem to induce in most writers a marked tendency to obscurantism. So use acronyms only when they are a positive aid to clarity.

Many staff do not, of course, have much experience of writing letters, reports or references to parents and employers, so it is reasonable for them to expect some help in advance, especially if their work is to be subject to criticism from above. The notes given to Halesowen staff on writing reports include the following:

1. INTRODUCTION
   Reports are obviously of the greatest importance, not least because they constitute a major public relations exercise for the college. The system of single subject slips should enable lecturers to give sufficient time to composing their comments without making the report period unduly long.

2. SOME PRACTICALITIES
   (i) Use a college blue or black biro so as to enable other colleagues to make minor corrections without referring back.

3. COMPILATION
   (i) The student's name is always to be given as first name, surname in that order.
   Ensure names are correctly spelt.
   (ii) If your signature is not easily legible, print your name next to it.
   (iii) Make sure all parts of the slip are completed.
   (iv) Try to make comments both encouraging and constructive.
   Write legibly – or type. Use a simple, direct but literate style. Avoid gobbledegook, latinisms and prissiness. And do get the spelling right!

And on writing references, the briefing paper contains the general points given below:

1 Use a simple, direct and brief style.
2 Avoid using the student's name more than once or twice – there is nothing wrong with pronouns.
3 The reference is collective; when the first person is used it must be 'we' not 'I'.
4 The reference must NOT be too long to fit the space – UCCA and PCAS[3] do not allow the use of continuation sheets. If it is too long, it will have to be sent back, thereby causing considerable delay.
5 Do include reference to any personal circumstances that are relevant, e.g. a bereavement, serious accident or illness, father made redundant.
6 Do not fear to be candid: references are immune from libel provided only that they are written in good faith. And, in any case, they are in the principal's name.
7 If possible give evidence for your assertions and expand on them.
8 Ensure your statements mean something to the reader. 'Above average' is a fairly useless phrase; 'above average for someone of university potential' is much more specific and helpful.
9 Sign and date your draft – we must know who drafted it and when.

Staff appointments

Communicating information plays a crucial part in appointing staff, from the written information in advertisements and the further details sent to applicants, to the way in which the selection process itself is organized. The aim is simple: to attract the largest number of suitable applicants and to appoint the best. The college is unlikely to be a free agent in this; the local authority and the governors may well have to be persuaded to alter their established procedures.

The advertisement needs to be brief, while communicating something of the style of the college as well as of the nature of the post, and it should invite those interested to ask for more information rather than to apply on the basis of the advertisement alone. And their enquiries need to be to the college, not the local education authority, or the personal touch essential to our concept of a college is lost.

The Halesowen internal guidelines for appointing staff are set out in our staff guide as follows:

1   Draft advertisement to be approved by the principal.
2   Authority asked to place advertisements in, among other places, appropriate ethnic press.
3   Information sheets to be approved by the principal.
    Advertisements and information sheets to contain the following statement on equal opportunities: 'Halesowen College is an equal opportunities college. We welcome applications from all suitably qualified people regardless of gender, ethnic origin, sexual orientation, age or disability.'
4   Applicants must be asked, in accordance with Dudley policy, to state ethnic origin.
5   Applicants to be sent a handbook and other appropriate college publications, circulars and minutes.
6   If an application form is used, it must be approved by the principal in advance. Irrelevant information, e.g. marital status, must not be requested.
7   Normally one referee is sufficient, but applicants should be allowed to nominate more if they wish. The head of the applicant's present institution or firm should normally be one of these.
8   Shortlisted candidates should be invited to come at different times. The schedule for each should normally be:
    (a) Report to Block 1 Reception;
    (b) Tour of college with one or more guides, who may be staff or students, (The SU have gladly agreed to this and they, or the student liaison officer, should be asked to provide guides), lasting for about ¾ hour.
    (c) Informal meeting with section or department (½ to 1½ hours).
    (d) Formal interview or other appraisal.

Afterwards each candidate leaves, being told that they will be contacted by telephone within a few days. Appointment agreed over the telephone is confirmed in writing with a reply slip accepting the appointment. Unsuccessful candidates are also notified in writing, usually telling them who is appointed.

9   Interviews can well be spread over more than one day, thereby obviating the need for marathon interviewing sessions.

10 The composition of the interviewing panel should be agreed with [the principal] – normally [he or she] will sit on it only if it is for an L2, SO IV or above.

11 Candidates to be told in advance of the procedure for the post they are applying for.

We try to avoid inviting all the candidates at the same time with each being interviewed while the others wait outside and the winner being announced in the presence of all the losers. We used to, but were persuaded to change by an article in *New Society* in, I think, the autumn of 1985. The writers persuaded us that this practice is often felt to be humiliating to the unsuccessful candidates. And it can happen that someone wants a day or two to think over before knowing for certain whether they want the post. The only loss is that one does not have the chance to offer a debriefing interview with the unsuccessful candidates as a way of helping them with their future applications.

It will be noted that students play a part in the procedure; and we do attach importance to the impression made by candidates on their student guides. And we also attach great importance to the feelings of those with whom the successful candidate will work. This not only improves the likelihood of appointing a person who will get on with their colleagues, but it also makes these colleagues committed in advance to making the appointment work, if it is, as it usually is, of someone they recommended. In practice, sections seldom recommend only one candidate; more often they suggest any of three or four, and we have no difficulty in choosing one of them.

In our advance information to short-listed candidates, we send a copy of the latest editions of the handbook and of various other college publications. All candidates, therefore, get a statement of the college aims. Of course.

Notes

1. See Sir Ernest Gowers, *The Complete Plane Words*, HMSO 1986.
2. For a discussion of the academic board, see Chapter 10, pp. 162–165.
3. UCCA is the central admissions agency for universities; PCAS for polytechnics.

Decision-making

A management system for a tertiary college needs to be more than a network of chains of command and of delegated tasks. It must also embody and exemplify principles that are fundamental to the college. And, like everything else, it has in addition an educational function for the students.

Inherent principles: management style

The structure of responsibilities is commonly, and disparagingly, referred to as the hierarchy. Significantly, for a hierarchy originally described rule by an ordered priesthood, and it was of its essence to be shrouded in mystery. In the college it is equally essential that government should be open. There must be no mystery surrounding management, and any priestly proclivities of senior staff must be suppressed.

And, despite salary scale being related to position in the management structure, it must be proclaimed that the structure is one of function not esteem. It exists to serve the purposes of the college, not to determine the degree of deference afforded to individuals. If senior staff are not to be priests, they must not be allowed to become mandarins instead.

In addition to being open, the management of the college must be accessible to influence from all its members. If the college belongs to the students and staff, they must be able to play a part in the decisions that shape it. So a management system must embody procedures for consultation. And for communication, for unless you are informed you cannot genuinely be consulted or advise.

A management system embodying these features is one that every college member contributes to; and there is, therefore, a sense in which all are members of the system. Attempts to divide the college into two discrete groups, management and the rest, which might be made, for example, at times of official union action, are potentially destructive of college unity, and all concerned should take care to conduct themselves in a way that does not allow this to happen.

There is another side to this coin. If all teachers are to be managers, all managers need to be teachers. The senior staff, including the principal, should therefore do some teaching, even if it is only an hour or two a week. Not to keep in touch with students, nor to prove they still can, nor even to retain an understanding of what it is like, valuable as all of these are; but to demonstrate by their actions commitment to the concept of a college without division between managers and workers – a workers' cooperative in fact. And the senior staff must not spend their lives behind the intimidating doors of their offices: a substantial part of their time must be spent walking around the college talking to students, staff and visitors – including uninvited ones! Of course this makes them harder to find, but intelligent use of internal telephones, or even a bleep system, can reduce the problem. The important point is that senior staff need to see and be seen if they are to remain effectively demystified. They can also do a lot to set the tone of the college by the manner in which they go about, setting an example of courtesy by holding doors open for students and staff, for example. And although senior staff bear considerable and ever-increasing burdens of administration which are vastly greater than their school equivalents have and which demand long hours at their desks in college and at home throughout the year, the time walking round college is not irrelevant to this. Often a highly relevant thought will occur as one walks around and, if scribbled down in a notebook, can save administrative time later.

It is not that the management system is in itself unimportant; it certainly is important, and various types will be discussed below. But it is not sufficient to have a good system; it must also be operated in a way that squares with the aims of the college. And the formal system is not merely a structure of delegated responsibilities; it must also include the overlapping aspects of structures of communication and of consultation and advice.

While an existing management system can be improved by

opening it up along the lines indicated, attitudes of staff set in their ways may make this difficult to achieve without the rude awakening of a complete restructuring. And that might be politically impossible. The real opportunity comes when a new college is formed by a school and college reorganization. The chance must not be lost.

Management structures

What system is best? The two main ones on the market are known as the 'departmental' and the 'matrix', although any college would probably claim to have modified the system they have chosen.

The departmental system is the traditional FE one. The college is divided up into departments corresponding to broad areas of the curriculum: engineering, business and secretarial, humanities, mathematics and science, and so on. Each department then operates semi-automonously, allocating its own budget, recruiting its own staff and students. Student hours are computed for each department separately and the salary of the department head and the number of lecturers at higher grades are determined by the total student hours. The system has great strengths. It enables effective devolution to a smaller and more comprehensible unit; and responsibility for teaching and caring for the student are combined. But the autonomy of the departments can militate against the college functioning effectively as a whole. This is especially the case as far as the ability of the college to offer courses spanning more than one department is concerned. It can also operate against the offering of disinterested advice to potential students, as each department has a vested interest in getting applicants to join their department – in recruiting regardless of the interest of the student. I am not saying that all FE departments succumb to this, but it is surely not a good idea to have a system with this temptation built into it.

The matrix system completely removes any vested interest in recruiting to one's own department. But at a cost. Subject teams cover the whole college and there are separate teams for pastoral care. On a diagram the two types of team are usually represented by lines at right angles to each other. In appearance this resembles a matrix in mathematics – which is a rectangular array of numbers obeying certain rules of combination with other such arrays. The advantages of a matrix system are preventing departmental interest biasing advice, removing any impediment to a variety of combinations of subject, forming cross-college teams for the teaching of subjects. The disadvantages are that it is messy and that it separates pastoral care from academic organization.

It is, however, possible to modify a departmental system so that its disadvantages are reduced. The first thing to do is to remove the direct connection between student hours and the grade of the department. Student hours must be totalled for the college as a whole, not for the departments separately. Next, the department heads must each have major cross-college responsibilities and their salary grade can then be related to their overall responsibilities, not merely their departmental ones. As a final impediment to departmental empire building, student admissions must be centralized. And to ensure access to courses across more than one department there must be a college timetable. This is designed to maximize such access and is not merely a putting together of independently produced departmental timetables.

A system modified like this with the departmental heads forming the senior management team of the college so that they are each managers of the whole college first and of their own departments second, is undoubtedly a great improvement. But there is still one snag. It shows itself in what is known as servicing – when a department wants to mount a course but the teachers of one component are in another department. The department providing a teacher to a course in another is said to be servicing the course. The servicing department has no incentive to release the best staff or at the most suitable times. The servicing teacher is on loan to another department, and may be less inclined to do their best when away from seniors in their own department whose valuation of them will affect their promotion prospects.

All things considered, it is to the credit of staff in departmentally organized colleges that servicing works as well as it does. But it is an unsatisfactory arrangement. One way round it is for the department needing expertise to appoint its own staff. This leads to a number of isolated teachers around the college: the mathematician in the engineering department cut off from other mathematics teachers, for example.

An alternative approach is to start with subject teams covering the whole college, but instead of erecting a separate personal – tutor system quite independently, to group these subject teams into departments, with the new-style departments responsible for tutoring but lacking any of the autonomy of the old type. Provided one has a tutor system based on homogenous tutor groups, the subject teams are also teams of tutors and thus several of these teams make up a department. There will be anomalies, with some subject teams in more than one department, but this does not matter provided curriculum delivery is devolved to the subject teams. The department head can have a curriculum role in two ways: by being a member of the senior management team of the college, and by having an advisory function *vis-à-vis* the subject team heads in, or partly in, their department.

The relationship of the department head and the subject head can then be similar to that of a good local authority adviser to a school head or head of department: no direct power, but able to help, encourage, advise and act as a catalyst. A key to this is money. It needs to be allocated directly to the subject head. But the department head will have been consulted by the subject head on the bid made, will have advised senior colleagues on the strength of the case, and will be further consulted by the subject head when the actual allocation is made. Furthermore, it is perfectly reasonable to give the department head also a supervisory and coordinating function on the spending of subject allocations.

But the major function of the department head, within this new-style department, is to lead the tutor system and thus the FE combination of academic and pastoral is maintained.

This system has further strengths. Technician support can be organized by departments, as in the traditional system. But if an area without technician support develops a need for it that subject area can simply be moved into a department where it is available. In addition, there is no need to organize departments identically. Each can be organized as best suits the subjects areas contained within it.

There is one final point on such a departmental system: it may be necessary to call it something else, like a faculty system, in order to prevent any misconception that it is really an FE type departmental system.

The essential difference is that the power over curriculum matters enjoyed by the head of department in the old system has been moved, either downwards to the head of the subject team or upwards to the senior management team. The head of department still has influences; with the former as an adviser, with the latter as a member of the team. But not unfettered autonomy.

The academic board

Teachers joining the college from schools will find one novel feature of the management system: the academic board, with membership and powers laid down in the articles of government for the college. Chaired by the principal, the board will have all or most of the senior staff on it by virtue of their offices together with elected teaching staff representatives for each department (or equivalent) and of the staff as a whole. The only support staff will probably be the chief administrative officer – the head of the support staff – and the librarian. Almost certainly, there will also be one or two places reserved for elected student representatives. Its powers will be defined in the articles by a phrase such as: 'responsible for the oversight of the academic work of the college including curriculum planning, coordination and development, and arrangements for the admission and examination of students'. Careful reading of the articles may well be needed to discover whether this board has powers of decision or is merely advisory. The difference is crucial; but in a way that is, perhaps surprising.

It might be supposed that the causes of openness and participation by ordinary college members would best be served by giving real, executive, power to the academic board. Not so – and the reason is not difficult to divine. The articles of government will state that the principal is responsible for the internal management of the college and the governors for its general direction subject to the overall policy, including financial control, of the authority. This is a perfectly comprehensible chain of responsibility; but then to give a college committee, the academic board, apparently unfettered power of decision over curriculum, examinations and student admissions, as many articles of government do, is not.

An executive academic board is a rival power base to the principal, and, furthermore, one with power but not personal responsibility. Any principal, whether of despotic or democratic instincts, would see it as important to prevent the academic board being a source of erratically frustrating counter-power. And the means of curbing the board are readily to hand; for the articles make the principal the chair of the board as well as effectively able to control its agenda. One of the first things I was told by kindly FE principlas, on becoming an FE principal myself, was how to emasculate an academic board. Their own success in this was readily apparent, with agendas largely confining the board to the trivial – the allocation of reserved car park spaces for example. On the odd occasions when an important item got through the net, the governors would be discreetly lobbied so as to limit the damage. Hardly surprisingly, many such academic boards become disillusioned, groups such as students not bothering to be represented, and those who did come breaking off from internecine squabbling only for the purpose of ganging up on the principal.

All this may be something of a caricature; and it is true that making the academic board advisory does not guarantee harmony and effectiveness. But it certainly makes it more likely, especially if the traditional department system has also been abolished, for then there are no rival departmental-head barons who might be inclined to look on the academic board as a convenient arena for their private battles. The principal has nothing to fear and everything to gain from taking an advisory board seriously; and the board members, having, ultimately, only an advisory function, will realize that their influence depends on the quality of their advice, and be inclined to refrain from pettiness and to debate genuinely.

The articles of government for Halesowen College were deliberately reworded to remove executive power from the academic board, not in order to increase the untrammelled power of the principal but because it was felt that the board would in fact be *more* powerful.

Everything possible must be done to ensure the board is fully consulted on all matters within its remit; and certainly an item must never be omitted from its agenda on the grounds that comments might be unwelcome. And the board's own procedures must be both efficient and open. The board will probably need to meet about once a month in term time, with meetings lasting two to three hours. The agenda and supporting papers need to be circulated widely well in advance so that those concerned about particular items can have time to lobby their representatives. Raising matters at short notice inhibits lobbying and thereby undermines participation in decision-making. 'Any other business' should not, therefore, appear on the agenda. For urgent matters a procedure involving a request signed by a given number of board members and submitted at least an hour before the meeting starts can be used. Meetings should be open to any college member to attend for all or part. Tickets in advance can enable the organizers to ensure the meeting is held in a room large enough to accommodate all the spectators.

Because minutes must be confirmed at the next meeting before being published, it is important to put out an 'unofficial' account of meetings immediately afterwards, with copies on staff and student boards. The same device is useful for governors' meetings. Confirmed minutes should go to management team and to governors, and be treated as of some considerable importance. Their going to governors affords an opportunity for staff and student representatives to question the principal on any occasion when the board's advice is not accepted. Although the board is only advisory, for its advice not to be taken should be a rare event requiring special explanation.

Non-board members should be encouraged to raise matters directly by submitting papers, and when the board discusses them, the author of the paper should be coopted on to the board for that item.

For many matters the board will need to set up sub-committees, either semi-permanent or of short duration. The former could cover such areas as the library, admission of students, staff in-service training, equal opportunities (by ethnic origin, gender, social class and physical disability); the latter, arrangements for the next open day, health education or the report system. All sub-committees should coopt a substantial proportion of non-board members, and all should report in writing to the board at prescribed times – they must not be set up, become forgotten and fade away.

Although the board is to advise on all major policy matters, it must not become all-embracing, and there must be other channels for college members to raise matters that are not major academic policy. The students' union committee[1] should meet the principal or a vice-principal to make complaints and requests.

Similar avenues are needed for the staff, and it is probably best to have two, one for support and one for teaching staff. Membership should be by election from each department, or equivalent, in the college. While meetings should be widely publicized so that all with complaints can tell their representatives of them, agendas in advance are undesirable as they would tend to inhibit items being raised. The main function of the principal at meetings of these bodies is to make notes and refrain from comment until the next meeting when a report of changes made or the reason why none is possible can be given. Although the style of management will encourage individuals to make complaints and suggestions directly, it is unlikely in the extreme that everyone will have the candour and courage to act individually, and the reassurance of a formal, and, if preferred, anonymous, channel of communication will be valued by many.

The existence of several unions for both support and teaching staff, with mutual suspicions and jealously-guarded privileges, probably makes it impossible to have union representation of the staff consultative committees. A pity. But in any event, the unions must have quick access to the top on any matters affecting a member's salary or conditions of service.

The senior management team

The top itself is, in law at any rate, the principal, who wields great powers subject only to the relatively unstructured constraint of governors and of the local authority. Virtually all principals will in fact set up a management team to advise on decisions for which they are responsible but could not possibly have the knowledge to take unaided. The management team will also have the effect of circumscribing the principal's power. And quite right too: all power corrupts etc.

The management team should comprise the principal, vice principals, heads of department (or assistant principals as we call them at Halesowen) and the chief administrative officer. Being the senior advisory body in the college, ranking even above the academic board, it is of great importance that it should be organized conspicuously well and very much in accord with the principles on which the college is based.

Meetings will need to be at least monthly and last for about two or three hours. An agenda must be published in advance, so that everyone knows what is going on and can express opinions if they wish. Minutes should be published, immediately after confirmation at the next meeting – people do not want to be kept waiting for weeks to find out what was decided – and copies put on staff and student notice boards; but for reasons of confidentiality it may occasionally be necessary to excise parts, with the full version, of course, sent in confidence to management team members.

It is of crucial importance that the agendas should be respected and that management team meetings should discuss only matters of policy. It is tempting to use them for detailed planning of particular events or for a general exchange of information. Either will undermine the purpose of having a management team as well as almost certainly boring some members of the team. A good general rule is that any discussion that fails to retain the attention of every member probably should not take place in the meeting at all.

Who should do the minutes? At Halesowen, after trying various alternatives, we have come to the view that the principal is the best person. S/he can dictate a version into a dictaphone immediately after each meeting and their secretary, being also the senior secretary, is the best person to type them up in view of the need for confidentiality.

Confidentiality also precludes allowing other college members to attend as observers, but for particular items individual colleagues can, with advantage both attend and take part. However, decisions should not be announced until after they have left or the status of management team would be compromised. Indeed, on occasion the principal would be well advised not to make a decision until after further reflection.

All advice tendered by other bodies, academic board, the students' union and the consultative committees for support and teaching staff, should be considered by the management team both because it is right that it should be and because doing so will encourage members of these bodies.

The management team stands at the apex of the system of consultation and advice: it also comprises the top layers of the system of delegated tasks and responsibilities. It has been argued earlier in this chapter that departments can be retained provided the departments serve the college and not vice versa. One aspect of this is that the heads of department must look on themselves as college managers first and departmental heads second. To that end, and for reasons of college unity, they need to have major cross-college responsibilities. Those that are not dependent on specialist expertise should be rotated over the years both for the sake of those who discharge them and as a demonstration that the senior team are managers of the college as a whole. Titles can also help attitudes, and at Halesowen we at first called the third-tier managers heads of faculty and now have renamed them assistant principals. This is a much better designation but one which proved very difficult to get through governors for reasons that were entirely to do with local politics and the fear that the other political party would make the accusation that the college was top heavy, despite the fact that only a name change was proposed, not an increase in posts.

The actual areas of responsibility that are delegated merit no discussion beyond that already given about the virtue of having a modified departmental system rather than a matrix one. But the number of people in each tier is important, especially at the more senior levels. It is curious that large schools commonly have three or four deputy heads while even larger FE colleges often have only one vice principal. In this respect, the school practice is vastly preferable. The difference stems from the different regulations: Schools Regulations allowing three or more deputies, FE Regulations discouraging more than one. It may seem remarkable that the Department of Education and Science should not be stimulated into enquiring which is the better, one or many deputies, and then bringing both sets of regulations into line on this. To those with experience of the DES it seems less remarkable. But deplorable nevertheless. A single deputy will either do everything or nothing. For delegation consists of dividing some of one's responsibilities and giving a share to each of a number of others. With one deputy this is impossible. So the minimum number for a system of delegation is two. With two vice-principals, each can undertake a general responsibility for half the managerial tasks of the college and subdivide them further between the department heads or assistant principals who are under them.

This is not to imply that the individuals actually perform tasks on their own. Everything should be done with others, in small teams. The conventional inverted pyramid representation of a management structure misses this out. A diagram showing how tasks are actually discharged, rather than the pattern of delegated responsibilities, would be a multitude of interlocking circles, each one representing a team doing something and overlapping other circles to show that many staff are in more than one team. Some teams will be semi-permanent; others will last for only a week or two while a particular event, say, is organized.

There are, however, three respects in which the inverted pyramid diagram is accurate. First, at each level the person concerned will retain charge. Second, each person in the pyramid will need a designated deputy so that things do not grind to a halt if someone is unexpectedly absent. Understudying is also an essential part of career preparation, and all staff need to be given the chance of gaining wider experience within the college. And third, there must be accountability; and the pyramid shows clearly who is above each person and, therefore, to whom each person is immediately accountable.

It is, of course, essential that all staff know who does what. So the system of delegation must be published. The Halesowen handbook has a brief general statement on the management of the college, with full details taking up thirteen pages in the staff guide.

Governors and parents

By Act of Parliament, every college and school in the public system must have a board of governors, with the proviso that smaller schools may be grouped under one board. The LEA has to draw up the legal charter for each governing body, called the instrument and articles of government, and have them approved by the secretary of state. Rather curiously, most attention has been given to the membership of governing bodies, not their powers.

Governors usually meet only once or twice a term, and most heads and principals look on them as a body representing the community generally and to which they have a duty of accountability. Their specific powers are to make or confirm staff appointments and to determine the curriculum. The latter is usually a dead letter – MSC normally ignore governors – but their role in appointing the head and senior staff is crucial, and can be disastrous.[2]

Colleges under FE Regulations normally have one or two representatives of the teaching staff on the governors, but seldom parent, student or support staff representatives. Tertiary colleges should. Halesowen College has two teaching staff representatives, one support staff, two students, two parents and one partner-school headteacher. But there is a firm majority of councillors from the ruling party or their nominees.

In 1986 a new act of parliament, the Education (No 2) Act 1986, changed the composition of school governing bodies to increase the number of parent representatives. It also gave wider powers to the governors over the curriculum. But no student or pupil governors at all were allowed.[3] In addition, school governing bodies were required to prepare an annual report to parents and a general meeting for parents must be held once a year at which the report is presented and the head, governors and local authority open to questions from parents about the report.

Tertiary and FE colleges are excluded from all these requirements,[4] but given that tertiary colleges aim to combine the best of both school and FE practices, they need to consider whether obligations similar to those imposed on schools by the Act should not be assumed voluntarily.

I think they should, and I recommended to my governors, at the meeting at the end of June 1987, that we increase the number of parent governors to five, the maximum specified under the Act for the largest school or sixth-form college. I also recommended the adoption of the practice of an annual governors' report to parents and a special meeting of parents at which it is discussed. As with schools, all parties concerned with the running of the institution would need to be present and answer questions. In addition to the principal, the governors and officers of the LEA, the MSC would also need to be represented. This would be entirely in the spirit of the Act, and if it is desirable for the principal, governors and LEA to have this sort of direct accountability to parents, there can surely be no objection to applying this also to the MSC. However, education officers and councillors were clearly soured by their experience of applying the Act to schools, where a great deal of work had resulted in only a handful of parents attending for the special meeting. Student representatives, supported by others, also opposed my recommendations on the grounds that an increase in parental involvement was inconsistent with treating students like adults. They were rejected. As it turned out two months later, the government had other plans anyway.

Setting objectives

Much of the discussion so far has been about how decisions should be made or tasks performed, not what these decisions and tasks should be. In general terms, of course, these are predetermined in the college aims, the requirements of the local authority and examination boards, and the expectations of the public.

These determine the general direction, but in most cases not the particular paths to be followed. It has not been usual in this country for schools and colleges to go into much detail about particulars, to draw up lists of objectives or publish development plans. Many feel that the performance of schools and colleges can be significantly improved by doing so. Others[5] argue that educational aims and objectives are more complex than the simple profit motive of a firm, and therefore that setting objectives and assessing success in achieving them are appropriate in the commercial world but not in the educational.

The argument is no longer academic. Government intervention in education through the MSC and various projects, most notably TVEI,[6] is compelling formal planning for the parts of the curriculum funded through these projects. This trend seems certain to continue and cannot be ignored.

It is of the greatest importance that a school or college should not present a one-sided account of its objectives or plan parts of the curriculum in isolation from the rest. For better or for worse, schools and colleges must engage in formal planning, and be prepared to publish, every year or two, a plan for the next few years.

Of course, the plan must be formulated in a way that is in accord with the aims and ethos of the college. That means it must not be compiled exclusively at the top and issued to everyone else as a set of orders. Instead, the plan itself must be produced by consultation involving the whole college, including governors, parents and employers. It must begin with the aims and then list objectives for the forthcoming year for the whole college. There is a considerable temptation to be influenced in what to list as objectives by what can be measured or quantified. This would be quite wrong. The validity of an objective is not in any way reduced if it proves hard to quantify progress towards it. Objectives must be formulated entirely independently of such considerations. If some turn out to be capable of statistical measurement so be it; but they are not, on that account, superior to those that do not.

The point of setting objectives is to improve performance in pursuing them. Assessment, or evaluation as it is usually called, of previous success is valuable only in so far as it helps future performance. Unless one knows what one is going to do with data there can be no point, other than idle curiosity in collecting it. It is simply not true that collecting data will, in itself, improve performance.

The objectives themselves must be medium-term aims that are neither trite nor generalized philosophy, and on which one can reasonably expect to make significant progress within a year, though not necessarily numerically quantifiable progress. It must also be remembered that the overwhelming majority of people-hours in the college are spent in teaching and learning, and the impression must not be given that only what happens outside a classroom is of importance.

With these caveats, formal planning can do much to reassure the outside world that the college knows what it is about and to gain renewed support for its work. It can also be a major unifying force in the college, as all are involved in setting objectives and are thereby seeing the aims as of continuing importance as they debate how to derive medium-term action from them.

Much of this chapter is not special to education. Management techniques apply to any organizaton. But the most technically perfect system in the world will fail if the people who comprise it lack commitment. It is by proclaiming its aims that a college does most to encourage the commitment, and leadership, at all levels, without which little can be achieved. And in so doing, it ensures not only that the management of the college promotes the aims but that it exemplifies them as well.

Notes

1. See Chapter 8, p. 133.
2. See Chapter 3, pp. 37–38, for a discussion of staff appointments by governors.
3. See Chapter 8, pp. 124–126, for a discussion of student governors and Halesowen College.
4. But in August 1987 the educational secretary announced, in a so-called consultative paper, his intention of radically changing the composition of governing bodies of FE colleges, including tertiaries, to put local employers in a majority. See also p. 83. The view of the government appears to be that parents must be in a majority for academic sixth-form colleges; employers and industrialists for FE colleges.
5. See, for example, Bernard Barker, *Rescuing the Comprehensive Experience*, Open University Press, 1986.
6. See Chapter 12, pp. 184–185.

PART SIX

The future

CHAPTER 11

At the crossroads

That Britain's last great reform of the education system should have been passed into law towards the end of the Second World War is less paradoxical than it might appear. Though the generals might have been looking no further ahead than final victory over the Axis powers, there were others, in all political parties and in none, who were determined this time, in contrast to the hollowness of the promise given by Lloyd George, the country's leader in the previous war, to build 'a land fit for heroes', that secure foundations would be laid for the future of the nation. Most of what came to be known at the 'Welfare State' was the result of reforms carried out by the post-war Labour government, although the groundwork had been done during the war by a small group of brilliant young men, including future Labour prime minister Harold Wilson, under the leadership of a lifelong Liberal, William (later Lord) Beveridge.

The 1944 Education Act, however, was steered through parliament by a Conservative, R. A. (later Lord) Butler, and will be forever associated with his name. Although it has lasted – albeit much amended – for over forty years, it was much more evolutionary than revolutionary, and in many ways was merely the last in a series of compromises, going back over a century, between the state and the voluntary providers of education – the churches, the independent schools, the universities. The system that had grown up was for public education to exist alongside that provided by local independent providers, who were at first a myriad of school boards with powers over elementary education only and were replaced in 1902 by local education authorities which were synonymous with counties or county boroughs.

While the 1944 Act strengthened the powers of LEAs, it did not nationalize education in the way that five years later the Labour minister Aneurin Bevan nationalized medicine, setting up the National Health Service and refusing to compromise with the doctors and consultants, so that the service was truly national in a way that education was not, and is not. Had it been a Bevan who reformed education, we would not have suffered the malign effects of a private system that separated out the classes and divided society, as well as ensuring that the wealthy, influential and articulate would show little interest in the public system as their children went to private schools (perversely called public schools).

The Act laid down, for the first time, that there should be a minister of education whose duty it should be

> to promote the education of the people of England and Wales and the progressive development of institutions devoted to that purpose, and to secure the effective execution by local authorities, under his control and direction, of the national policy for providing a varied and comprehensive education service in every area.

Remarkably, the clause lay dormant, as a sort of time bomb, for some forty years, and real power over what happened in schools and colleges slipped away from the minister.

Because it was a compromise with the voluntary providers, the Act specified only one subject in the school curriculum, religious education.[1] And nothing at all was laid down about the curriculum in a college under FE Regulations. Control of the curriculum was vested, for each school and college, in its governing body, subject to the general policies of the local education authority. Governing bodies were made up of nominees of the local council, various categories of coopted members and, possibly, elected representatives of staff, parents and pupils or students. Local political parties were generally adept at ensuring that every governing body had a firm majority of the locally ruling party, but few governing bodies had much idea of what powers they had or how they ought to go about exercising them.

The charter for each school and college, consisting of two documents called the instrument of government and the articles of government, had to be approved by the education authority. It was normally specified that governors were responsible for the curriculum and the head for internal management and discipline. The interest of governors usually led to their discussing *only* the latter, never the former. Heads liked this as it kept governors out of the curriculum, thereby leaving the most important part of the school or college to them, subject only to the local authority being prepared to provide the necessary teachers. And local authorities often allocated teachers on the basis of one for a given number of pupils, with little regard for the subjects they would teach. So, with the governors and the local authority opting out, and the government having no statutory powers anyway, what was taught in the nation's schools and colleges was in the effective control of heads and principals, with the external examining boards being the only constraint. These quasi-autonomous bodies exercised considerable influence, weakened only by the fact that schools and colleges could sometimes shop around to find an examination to their liking. Until 1987, for ordinary school subjects there were two main examinations, GCE at O and A level, and CSE, with eight GCE and fourteen CSE boards. In 1987, O levels and CSEs were merged to provide a single examination at sixteen, the General Certificate of Secondary Education (GCSE), leaving the GCE boards responsible for A levels at eighteen. Five GCSE boards were formed from the former CSE and O level boards. At the same time the government embarked on a rationalization of vocational qualifications, which would affect boards such as the Business Technician Education Council (BTEC), the City and Guilds Institute of London and the Royal Society of Arts (RSA). A great deal of in-fighting developed between the various boards as each sought to secure a dominant position in the turmoil, and some almost bizarre edicts were issued, notably the one from BTEC in 1986 prohibiting a student from taking a BTEC National Certificate (of A-level standard) in conjunction with an A level.

During the 1970s and 1980s, visiting foreign educationalists were often incredulous, and British education ministers embarrassed, at the lack of central control, or even influence, over the curricula of the nation's schools and colleges. The frequency of ministers' embarrassment increased after the UK joined the European Community (EC) in 1974, and British education ministers began to take part in regular meetings with their European counterparts.

Successive education ministers fumed privately about their impotence and looked for ways of gaining control over the education system, but without the controversy that an act of parliament would provoke. The first significant inroads were made by a Conservative education minister, Sir Keith Joseph, in the early 1980s, by the device of withholding a small part[2] of the government's annual grant[3] to local authorities and using it to fund specific projects centrally. At roughly the same time the government greatly expanded the Manpower Services Commission (MSC) – originally set up in 1974 to plan the training needs of the nation as we entered the EC – and used it to influence directly what was happening in FE colleges, and to a lesser extent schools. From the mid-1980s a proportion of the government grant to local authorities designated for FE colleges, including tertiary colleges, was withheld and made available via the MSC, and on their terms. This gave the MSC enormous power, and local authority education officers and college principals were increasingly compelled to dance to the MSC tune. The theme was skill-training for specific jobs.

For the first half of the 1980s, the government persisted in the view that income from North Sea oil must not be used to finance public expenditure or 'room' would not be left for the rise of new manufacturing, a theory that is both curious and, ultimately, had the exact opposite of the intended effect.

During the same period, the rise in unemployment among the young coincided with a shortage of people with technological skills. Old-fashioned manufacturing industry declined rapidly, until by 1985 we were, for the first time in our history, a net importer of manufactured goods, and by the following year we were running a deficit on our balance of trade for manufactured goods of some £6 billion. This decline was an inevitable consequence of failure to invest in the previous three decades, but it was the lack of investment in education and training that was the major factor inhibiting the rise of new manufacturing to take the place of the old. Finance for investment in new technologies is not enough; there must also be sufficient workers with the necessary skills – and there were not. So very high unemployment existed alongside job vacancies in certain key occupations.

By early 1987 it was apparent not only that the Conservative government had abandoned its previous stance, but also that something of a political consensus was emerging on education. Suddenly it was again the received wisdom that education was a vital form of investment for the future. And while there were disagreements on particular policies, there were also many agreed objectives that had potentially far-reaching consequences: the need to improve skills training and retraining at all levels; the need to exercise a degree of government control over the curriculum in schools and colleges; relating teachers' pay to conditions of service and insisting on some form of appraisal of teachers' performance.

But the government still maintained a hostility to local education authorities, especially Labour ones, and government ministers lost no opportunity to heap scorn on the allegedly lunatic behaviour of a few left-wing Labour-controlled London authorities, usually citing tabloid press reports, often mendacious about foisting pro-homosexual and pro-black attitudes on schoolchildren. No matter that the majority of authorities, of whatever political complexion, were struggling as best they could to maintain a decent service with inadequate resources while bedevilled by inconsistent government policies. Many doubted whether local authorities would survive at all for much longer if the Conservatives were elected for a third term of office. This feeling was reinforced after the election of June 1987 with the government making clear that it intended to emasculate local authorities by allowing schools to opt out of local control altogether, to reduce LEA influence over FE colleges, and to introduce a national curriculum while squeezing LEA finances still further by outlawing the 'creative accounting' that had kept many afloat in previous years, in preparation for the replacement of the rates by a poll tax and a nationally determined business levy.

So, while recognizing the need to invest in education and training, the government was anxious to do so in a way that did not give increased power to the despised local authorities. The secretary of state, Kenneth Baker, spoke of devolution to the periphery of the wheel, by which he meant giving more control to school heads while bypassing the local authorities with grants for specific purposes. And soon after the 1987 election, he announced plans to do the same for FE, including tertiary, colleges, with the difference that they would be governed by local industrialists and expected to raise money by commercial deals and sponsorship.

At the same time long-overdue rationalization and reforms of public provision up to the age of nineteen seemed to be in danger of dividing young people into two distinct categories; the academic who would go on to A levels, or whatever succeeded them, at eighteen and then higher education, and the rest who would become full or part-time students at an FE college taking what were termed 'work-related' courses. Whether this dichotomy was a product of accident or design was less clear. The evidence of design included the reluctance of the MSC to have anything to do with A-level students at tertiary and FE colleges, the separate rationalizations of academic and vocational qualifications, the plan to set up city technology colleges as eleven-to-eighteen schools in cities, directly funded by government and local industry with the local authority totally excluded, and the different compositions of governing bodies for schools and FE colleges.

If the intention was to open up a divide between academic youngsters and the rest, then the forty or so tertiary colleges stand inconveniently in the way, providing not only for all types of sixteen-year-old, but also doing their best to integrate provision so as to blur the distinction between the theoretical and the applicable. And while the secretary of state continued to approve reorganizations involving the founding of tertiary colleges, he refrained, as had his predecessor, from saying anything supporting tertiary colleges in principle and at the same time often insisting, when approving proposals, on some school sixth forms continuing alongside the new college or colleges. Furthermore, the proposal to allow schools dissatisfied with the LEA to opt out and be funded directly by the DES if a majority of parents voted for this looked like making it impossible for any sixteen-plus reorganization to succeed. A school wishing to retain its sixth form would simply opt out, and as the LEA would be compelled to fund it, via the DES, at the previous rate, no economy would be achieved. So on the one hand the government was telling local authorities to rationalize provision so as to reduce the number of school places in line with the fall in rolls while on the other it was legislating to impede any action likely to have this effect.

In the absence of any general policy statement, the position of the Conservative government had to be inferred from its actions. By contrast, both the Alliance parties and the Labour Party publicly supported tertiary colleges in principle,[4] and this has been translated into action in at any rate some areas, even when it was not popular. In the Dudley Authority, for example, when Labour regained control in 1986 they changed a proposal for a sixth-form college to one for a tertiary college. To their credit, this was done not because it would win them any votes but because of their commitment to the tertiary college as comprehensive post-sixteen provision. In August 1987, after the usual infuriating and expensive delay by the minister, this plan was rejected, but the reasons given were not that he was opposed to a tertiary college but that too many small schools would be left. The Dudley education chair, Councillor Savage, drew the not unreasonable conclusion that small schools could be closed in Labour areas but not in Conservative ones. So even after the Conservative victory in the General Election of June 1987, the future of tertiary colleges was far from clear.

In the run-up to the 1987 election, the Conservatives promised a national curriculum for schools. Rather surprisingly, the Labour Party agreed. And although the Alliance only went as far as a national framework before the election, they too seemed unlikely to oppose a national curriculum afterwards.[4] The long-running and greatly damaging teachers' pay dispute ended with the fractious and poorly led unions alienating enough of the overwhelming public support they had started out with for Kenneth Baker, who became education secretary in 1986, to dare to pilot a bill through parliament allowing him to impose both pay and conditions on school teachers, but not college lecturers. This he promptly did, thus putting schoolteachers in the almost uniquely disadvantageous and humiliating position of not even being able to negotiate on their contracts of employment.

But if the schoolteachers had been put on a boat over which they had no control, the college lecturers appeared to have missed it altogether. There seemed a risk that their pay would fall significantly behind that of the their colleagues in schools, as the government seemed determined to refuse any additional funding for a pay settlement, as it had for schoolteachers, thereby leaving the LEAs, technically the employers, no alternative but to make any pay award self-financing. Thus, the government believed, the colleges would be compelled to toe the line of greater efficiency. Whether the supposed greater efficiency, by which they meant larger classes and longer staff hours, would be at the expense of quality remains to be seen. But with the lecturers' union, the National Association of Teachers in Further and Higher Education (NATFHE) in a weak bargaining position and enjoying little recognition, let alone support, there seemed little doubt about who was going to win.

In the period of post-war reconstruction it was commonly said that Britain had but two natural resources, coal and the innate abilities of its people. To exploit the latter, investment in education was seen as essential. Hence the expansion of higher education. Then came comprehensives and disenchantment with the nation's schools, which were generally blamed for a lack of respect for authority amongst the younger. So when another natural resource was discovered, oil, it became easy to neglect the need to exploit the human natural resource. And the version of monetarism that was inflicted on the British people after the 1976 financial crisis and intensified in 1979 included among its holy writ the tenet that the entire public sector was in some way parasitic on the wealth-generating private sector. At first the public sector had to be cut

back in order to effect a transfer of the work-force to the private
sector, then it was because the frontiers of the state had to be rolled
back, then because the public sector was indolent and inefficient
after years of soft living.

By 1987 oil revenues were beginning to decline. Monetarism had
produced lower inflation but at the cost of much higher unemployment, and the much vaunted private sector was complaining that
expansion was inhibited by a shortage of skilled labour. Investment
in education and training suddenly became a national priority
again, as it had been forty years previously; but with the very great
difference that a government had at last decided to take control of
the nation's education system and exercise power given to the
education minister in the 1944 Act which had lain dormant for so
long. The question was no longer whether to invest in education,
but how. And the government did indeed have the power to
choose between different options. And the importance of the
sixteen to nineteen age range was agreed by all.

Although Kenneth Baker, secretary of state for education and
science both before and after the 1987 election, avoided saying
anything about them, the future of tertiary colleges was fundamental to any strategy for post-sixteen provision.

Notes

1. The Education Act (No 2) 1986 did lay down certain general criteria
   for sex education and strengthen governor control over this subject.
   However, these provisions apply only to schools, not to colleges
   under FE Regulations.
2. 0.5 per cent when first introduced in 1974.
3. The income of a local council was mainly made up of a grant from
   central government and the receipts of a local property tax called 'the
   rates'. In 1980 the former was about 70 per cent of the total; by 1986 it
   had fallen to about 50 per cent. Furthermore, by then local authorities
   faced severe legal restrictions on the amount they could raise through
   the rates.
4. See Chapter 3, note 3 for the manifesto statements of the major parties
   in the 1987 general election, and Chapter 5, note 4, for the priorities of
   the parties on a national curriculum.

CHAPTER 12

Our best hope

By the late 1980s the trend towards separate colleges at sixteen appeared irresistible, and certainly irreversible, and to be running strongly in favour of tertiary rather than sixth-form colleges. But opposition from educationalists was not entirely stilled. Argument in the correspondence columns of *The Times* centred on whether Latin and French would be threatened by the removal of sixth forms from schools, with Laurence Norcross, headmaster of Highbury Grove, asserting that they would and Frances Morrell, then leader of the Inner London Education Authority, arguing the opposite, and in Latin at that (with a translation on another page just in case there were any *Times* readers who did not read Latin).

An article in the *Daily Telegraph* of 31 March 1987, entitled 'Goodbye to the School Sixth Form?' also provoked a letter from Mr Norcross, this time arguing that sixth forms were essential to good schools and that his in particular had massive local support which should not be ignored. The *Telegraph* article also quoted Michael Pipes headmaster of Portsmouth Boys' School and the 1987–8 president of the National Association of Headteachers, as saying that he was 'personally still haemorrhaging' from what he regarded as the decapitation of his school.

The two professional organizations for secondary headteachers, the Secondary Heads Association (SHA) and the National Association of Headteachers (NAHT), were in the slightly difficult position of having a small number of college principals amongst their members. No doubt this is why neither had a clear policy on colleges. Both published papers in 1987 on the fourteen-to-eighteen curriculum[1] which could be read as implying the necessity of retaining sixth forms in schools, but refrained from actually saying so, although the SHA paper did warn about 'the precipitous introduction of tertiary education 16–19 in many areas without sufficient consideration of the long-term implications for schools and education as a whole'.

It is undeniable that a number of minority subjects such as Latin have disappeared from many schools, but this can hardly be blamed on removing sixth forms from schools. As was shown in Chapter 1, by gathering together all the twos and threes doing a minority subject into an economically viable group, the college tends to preserve such subjects. It is, on the contrary, small sixth forms that pose the threat to subjects like Latin.

So much for Mr Norcross and his fellow *Times* correspondents. The fourteen-to-eighteen argument carries more weight. It is undoubtedly true that there are grave deficiencies in the present curriculum pattern based on an option system in the last two years up to sixteen. It too easily allows certain career avenues to be permanently closed and it does not allow a pupil to sample by taking a subject over a shorter period than two years. And with more and more continuing in full- or part-time education or training up to eighteen, there is a strong need to tie in the curriculum up to sixteen with that beyond.

In 1984 the government set up, through the MSC, the Technical and Vocational Education Initiative (TVEI), at first in a small number of pilot schemes, then, in 1986, making it available to all LEAs with a promise of funding for ten years. TVEI was not another examination; rather it was a way of getting a greater technical and vocational bias into the fourteen-to-eighteen curriculum. The MSC provided funding for local co-ordinators, staff training and equipment.

The notion that TVEI implies the retention of school sixth forms does not bear examination. The fact that only a minority can proceed to the sixth form is the flaw. A TVEI scheme in an area with school sixth forms necessitates coordination of fragmented sixteen-plus provision. Moreover, the schools will lack the level of technological equipment readily available in a college. It is little better where there is a sixth-form college, for again provision is inefficiently divided between the two types of post-sixteen college. It is only in a system comprising a tertiary college providing comprehensive post-sixteen education and its partner comprehensive – and special – schools that one gets the most efficient model. The writers of the NAHT and SHA booklets have made the erroneous assumption that curriculum continuity implies the same institution. Yet do they argue for schools for the five-to-eighteen age range?

The Halesowen TVEI scheme is a good example of what only a tertiary system can deliver. The college is working in partnership with the six eleven-to-sixteen schools which provide between them the bulk of its intake at sixteen and with a special school. TVEI will be for *all* their pupils in their last two years. The concentration of technological expertise and equipment in the college enables staff training to be done in the college by college staff. Equipment in the schools can then be bought to supplement what is available in the college, and all fourth- and fifth-year school pupils will go to the college for some sessions each week. And, most important of all, the teaching syllabuses in the schools and in the college are being determined jointly. The fact that, like other tertiary colleges, we already have effective liaison and a real sense of partnership makes this possible.

Rather surprisingly, there was little national debate among educationalists on the pros and cons of tertiary colleges. It was as if the war had been lost without a major battle having taken place or, indeed, any formal surrender having been made. And while the government might adopt an agnostic stance on the issue, it certainly did have policies that concentrated the minds of LEAs on reorganization. The government's financial watchdog, the Audit Commission, published a report in May 1986 after a detailed study of LEA school systems[2] and concluded that 1,000 schools needed to be closed in the following five years. But they did not say how this was to be done.[3]

To local authorities the message was clear: only if they made their education systems more efficient would they be able to spend more per pupil – or avoid spending less. And, as was shown in Chapter 1, that means, among other things, concentrating sixth-form provision, so there were few areas by the late 1980s which had not either set up colleges or were not contemplating doing so. Ten years previously the public response to any LEA which made such a suggestion would have been a blank wall of hostility. But by now there were differences.

While the old fondness for school sixth forms continued to flourish in 1987, the opposition to tertiary proposals was no longer monolithic. Many were inclined not to oppose tertiary colleges as such, but to ask questions about the tertiary college proposed for their area. Others, while lamenting proposals to remove sixth forms, positively demanded a good tertiary college as the only acceptable alternative. And some appreciated that a headmaster's attachment to his sixth form does not in itself guarantee that the sixth form is good for the sixth-formers in it.

But if it is no longer reasonable for the concerned parent, or indeed pupil, teacher, councillor or, simply, ratepayer, to be opposed to a local tertiary reorganization on principle, it would certainly be unreasonable to welcome *any* scheme that is labelled 'tertiary'. What then should one look for in a proposed tertiary reorganization? Drawing on what has been advocated in this book, we get the following checklist.

As the reorganization yields economies of scale, it is reasonable to expect the LEA to make a good proportion of the savings available at once. Not just to the new college, but to the schools also. Accommodation in both schools and college must be appropriate and of a good standard. Few areas will be as fortunate as Halesowen, with excellent new buildings not only for the college but also for two of the schools, and with the others having major building programmes. But why should this not become the norm? Such a programme is undoubtedly a worthwhile investment and should be demanded everywhere. For too long we have been prepared to accept second best in the education of our young people, and to house both them and those to whom we entrust their education in shabby and poorly furnished buildings. One result of our almost obsessive devotion to existing schools has been to resist closing schools even when standards of accommodation for all could be raised very considerably by doing so. If we are moving into a period when concern is for educational standards rather than the continuation of particular schools, we must all also ensure that standards are raised as a result of closures. Buildings, furniture and equipment would be a good place to start.

It is not only the standard of accommodation that is important; its location is also crucial. Split sites are to be avoided; and especially for the college, unless the sites are sufficiently close to allow the college to function as a unity. As has been shown in Chapter 3, a split site implies a significant loss of curriculum choice, and hence of the unique advantage of a tertiary college. At Halesowen our second campus is a mile away, and at some cost we run a minibus service between the two campuses and thereby avoid hiving off part of the curriculum. I would guess that more than three sites or a maximum distance between sites of more than two miles would be a worst case for a true tertiary college. While I have nothing but admiration for colleges that flourish with more separation than this, I am sure their principals would agree that no new colleges should be set up with that degree of separation.

Human resources are, of course, even more important. Staff, both teaching and support, must be handled with great sensitivity. A rigidly bureaucratic approach is likely to be disastrous. Nor must penny-pinching prevent the building up of effective teams in both college and schools. As was argued in Chapter 3, it is essential to have an outsider to head the new college, and there may well be other key positions where new blood is called for. This will undoubtedly cause some heartache, and expense in providing decently for those heads and others who are no longer needed, through no fault on their part.

Having got the right staff in place in both college and schools, it is crucially important to get them working together as soon as possible. Certainly the foundations of liaison must be laid before the college opens. A good deal is said about this in Chapter 2.

Staff relationships, both between the college and its partner schools and within the college, are obviously crucial. The new tertiary college should start with roughly equal numbers of teaching staff from schools and from further education. (If it does not, this is ground for suspicion of the whole reorganization.) One objection sometimes raised against tertiary colleges is that teachers or lecturers from such different backgrounds cannot hope to start with good professional relationships. There might be reason for fearing this if tertiary colleges were organized in two halves – schools and FE. But they are not, or certainly should not be. The internal organization of a tertiary college must ensure the college functions as a unit and that staff from both traditions are represented equally at all levels. And, of course, in their workings they must adopt the best practices from each of these traditions, so as to be neither a school nor an FE college but to incorporate the best of both to make a single institution that is better than either.

As has been argued in this book, a tertiary college has a unique opportunity to promote the character development of its students and to provide an education in partnership and working together with mutual respect between people of different abilities and interests that is almost literally of vital importance to the future of our nation. But not if the college is too large, or has too small a proportion of full-time students, or has too big a proportion of over-nineteen students. There is a difference between adolescents and adults, and while the tertiary college should pride itself on the adult atmosphere provided for its students, a college in which the dominant ethos is post-nineteen will not provide an appropriate atmosphere for adolescents. This is why tertiaries should not have many advanced (i.e. post-A-level) courses. Similarly, the proportion of full-time sixteen-to-nineteen students must be sufficient for this group to define the dominant ethos among daytime students – evening-only students being largely irrelevant to this argument. One of the challenges facing the tertiary as government policies, rightly, increase the number of part-time students of all ages, is to assimilate them without losing the corporate identity that is essential to the full-time sixteen- to nineteen-year-olds. And, as was argued in Chapter 3, around a thousand such full-time students seems about right.

In September 1986 there were about forty tertiary colleges in England and Wales, in twenty-four different LEAs. Yet the first sixteen colleges opened between 1970 and 1982, so the rate of going tertiary is increasing. So how are tertiary colleges doing? Are they living up to expectations?

Perhaps surprisingly, there were in 1987 no definitive answers to these questions. No objective appraisal had been carried out. The national education inspectorate, the HMI, carefully refrained from expressing any general view. Even the retired staff HMI who wrote, anonymously, the digest on tertiary colleges published in the respected magazine *Education* in July 1986 avoids any overall judgement, although he does assert that they have continued the FE tradition of providing both full- and part-time courses for all ages 'with great success', and he writes of their 'eventual cost-effectiveness'. But that is all. Anyone not versed in the fence-sitting tradition of the British Civil Service – and HMI are Civil Servants – might suspect that something is being concealed.

Not so. Although I can pretend to no comprehensive knowledge of tertiary colleges in general, all that I hear of other colleges is favourable, and the few I have visited are clearly doing well in all respects. Others, who have had more contact than I with various tertiary colleges, confirm my impression. And there is plenty of opportunity for contact. The Tertiary Colleges Association (TCA) is active in promoting a continous exchange of ideas between not only staff but also education officers and governors. In addition to issuing regular bulletins, the TCA organizes an increasing number of conferences each year. In 1987, for example, Halesowen alone acted as host to two TCA conferences.

When a reorganizaton is mooted, fears are usually expressed, reasonably enough, that the presence of vocational students will prevent the development of an academic atmosphere similar to that to be found in school sixth forms, thereby reducing academic success. Again there are no national statistics of examination success, but such evidence as there is suggests the opposite and that colleges do better at A level and university entrance than the sixth forms they replace. That has certainly been our experience at Halesowen, and, as was shown in Chapter 2, it was the view of government ministers as well.

Parents facing a reorganization affecting their children could be forgiven for feeling punch-drunk; some will have had children caught up in reorganization, re-reorganization and even re-re-reorganization. In some areas grammar and secondary modern schools were replaced by a system of primaries up to age ten, middle schools for ten- to thirteen-year-olds followed by senior high schools for those over thirteen or fourteen. A few years after that the middle schools were abolished, and a year or two later sixth-form provision concentrated in a college, which in turn was replaced by the amalgamation of sixth-form and FE colleges to form tertiary colleges. Recent times have also seen a major reorganization of local government, as well as two years of teacher disruption. Many children have been caught up in two or more of these upheavals, and some have been affected by four of them.

Every one of the many different ways of organizing public education from five to nineteen was thought at the time, at any rate by some, to be the last word. So if parents are to feel any confidence that tertiary colleges are here to stay, it must be demonstrated not only that they suit present conditions but that they will suit all foreseeable future ones as well. Given that the one certainty is that circumstances will change, this entails showing that the tertiary college is both stable and adaptable. And not only the tertiary college, but the whole system of schools and college as well. To do this it must be shown that the system can cope with all projected developments, and that there are no foreseeable changes which it cannot assimilate. In fact, as I hope to show in the concluding section of this book, an even stronger claim can be made, namely that the tertiary system is not only the best to implement likely changes; it is the only system that can.

In an article in *The Independent* of 5 May 1987, the former editor of *The Times* wrote: 'The economic change of recent decades has been from the primacy of manufactures to that of communications, from machine power to electronic power, from factory to office, from mass production to small teams.' Rees-Mogg calls our new economic era 'the electronic age'. It is clearly already upon us, and equally clearly is going to be a period of ever-increasing and unending technological change. The implications for education are enormous. Some changes are happening already, more are likely in the fairly near future. Let me attempt to list some of them.

First and foremost is the impact of the computer. It is now recognized that the old division between those who worked with their brains and those who worked with their hands is no longer valid. The computer puts an enormous extension of mental power at the disposal of everyone. Everyone needs to be a computer literate.

But we must not fall into the trap of supposing that manipulative dexterity with a keyboard in front of a VDU is sufficient. It is not. There must be understanding as well, not so much of how a computer works but of what it can be made to do, and its power to deal with information. The electronic age is the age of information processing. Information technology is here to stay; and it has the potential to magnify the power of the mind as, analogously, mechanical tools magnified the capabilities of human muscle. We are tool-making animals. First we invented mechanical tools to increase our physical powers, now our electronic tools increase our mental powers. Their potential is almost literally mind-blowing. What the future holds we cannot possibly know. But we can and do know what needs to be done in the curriculum of our schools and colleges – information technology for all. And all must include both sexes. We are desperately short of high-level mathematicians, scientists and technologists. Yet the female half of the population represents a virtually untapped pool of ability. It is a matter of the utmost urgency that this pool is tapped, both for the sake of the nation and for the sake of the thousands of women who are still conditioned to underachieve. The new technology is removing the image of the engineer as a man in oily overalls with a wrench in one brawny hand. There is nothing specifically masculine any more about science or its applications, and the quicker this is generally appreciated the better.

The curriculum for the more intellectually able is in urgent need of reform. The present A-level system is little short of a disaster. To the incredulity of other advanced nations, we allow large proportions of our ablest young people to drop mathematics, science, foreign language or study of their own language at the age of sixteen. A levels should be replaced by a system of five or more subjects in which everyone must continue studying the four subject areas just listed.

There is an equally important need to change the system of financial support after the age of sixteen. At the moment our system of unemployment benefit has the effect of giving a financial inducement not to undergo education or training. And it makes no more sense to pay young people to undergo training on YTS but not education. In any case, the separation of education from training is a totally outdated concept, and the government needs to merge education and training in a new department of state.[4]

A trend that is clearly here to stay is the increase in part-time education. Allied with this are developments in what are called curriculum modules. These are self-contained courses of relatively short duration. Each module can be of six to twelve weeks for three or so hours a week. At the end the student is assessed and given a credit. Credits can be collected until there are sufficient for, say a GCSE or an A level. Some courses will require specific credits as entry qualifications. We need to develop greatly the validity of credits right across the whole academic–vocational spectrum, not merely across the vocational end as is being done currently by the National Council for Vocational Qualifications. More and more curriculum modules for students in the fourteen-to-eighteen age range will need both academic and vocational elements. A tertiary college working with the partner schools can ensure this curriculum breadth; other systems cannot.

In all these curriculum developments, the tertiary system is at an advantage. To divide post-sixteen provision into two colleges, sixth-form and FE, means that either everything must be duplicated or some opportunities will be denied in each college. Everyone needs access to the whole range. The breaking down of the irrelevant and harmful academic–vocational divide can only be achieved if we put both elements in the same institution – a tertiary college.

The tertiary college is, then, the most efficient and effective way of educating the population for the new electronic age. But while a prime aim of education must be to give people the skills to promote economic prosperity and social harmony, it is not the most important aim. What distinguishes a liberal democracy is that ultimately it puts the individual before the state. There is more to life than information technology.

Human beings are neither computers nor automata. Everyone also needs to come into contact with the creative arts. Indeed the more our technology advances, the more vital it is to cultivate the artistic, creative and spiritual dimensions of human existence. Again it is only the tertiary college that is likely to be able to offer experience in these to everyone.

Above all the tertiary college provides, as I hope I have shown, a unique opportunity for people to learn to work together, recognizing differences in abilities and interests but respecting each other as people. After the age of sixteen this can happen only if all full-time students are in the same college and not separated out from those on different types of course. But it does not finish with the full-time students. As the number of part-time students increases – as it will – they must be fused into the same college and learn the same lessons of working together as do the full-time students. Indeed there must be an equality of college membership for all categories of student. Everyone gains, full- as well as part-time. Historically a new college will probably define its aims and set its standards with the full-time students, but these aims and standards must then be extended to the part-time students. Some part-timers will be a good deal older. This is a positive advantage, and the presence of older people in classes and common rooms enhance the adult atmosphere.

In the United Kingdom a considerable amount of separating out occurs at all ages as a consequence of the flourishing independent sector. In 1987, 7 per cent of all pupils under the age of sixteen were in independent schools, but of A-level students the proportion was 17 per cent. If one accepts my arguments for comprehensive education both pre- and post-sixteen, the independent sector represents a major weakness in the nation's education system. Yet the willingness of parents to pay for what they see as being better schooling for their children is both laudable and their right. I do not see how one could condemn the motives of these parents or make independent schools illegal. They could be made more expensive by removing the tax concessions they enjoy and abolishing the Assisted Places Scheme under which the government subsidizes the school fees for poorer families whose children win places to an independent school. But this would merely make the independent sector more exclusively the preserve of the rich.

Most independent schools are substantially better housed and equipped than state schools, but this is partly a consequence of the articulate and influential not having their own children in the latter. And the Assisted Places Scheme uses government money that would otherwise be available to the state schools.

Many, but by no means all, independent schools provide a better education than most state schools do, but I believe nevertheless that the existence of the independent sector has been, and is, profoundly harmful, not only in weakening the state sector but also in accentuating and perpetuating class-divisions. These class-divisions are largely responsible for our inability to pull together, for the generally poor relationships between bosses and workers and for the low level of competence that has been the distinguishing characteristic of British management, where connections rather than ability have been the pasport to promotion.

To someone who values the freedom of the individual, there is only one acceptable way to weaken the independent sector: make the state sector more attractive. Under Conservative governments this might be thought virtually impossible, as they have steadily squeezed the state sector of the level of funding necessary to maintain standards as numbers fall. Nevertheless, both sixth-form and tertiary colleges report significant numbers of entrants at sixteen from independent schools. The superiority of the independent sector is nothing like so great after sixteen as it is up to sixteen. So perhaps the move to tertiary colleges will do something to draw together those outside the state system as well as those within it.

There remains one claim made for the existence of an independent sector: choice. Bernard Levin wrote in *The Times* on 1 June 1987: 'There is a very powerful movement to abolish all choice in education … and force all parents (*sic*) through the narrow gate that leads to uniformity, and the narrow gate beyond it that leads to inadequate standards.' He has a point. Lack of choice would lead to monopoly providers, and could lead to complacency and lower standards of teaching, student motivation and learning, which is why I applaud the Conservative government's abolition of catchment areas for schools and for colleges. All post-sixteen provision should be in tertiary colleges, but tertiary colleges need to be kept on their toes by competition with others. That is one reason why they should not be large. For competition will only work if colleges are sufficient close together for a good proportion of students to be able to choose between more than one.

The only post-sixteen institutions that need to remain separate are those of higher education – universities and polytechnics. In this the dominant ethos is currently that of the nineteen- to twenty-two year olds who form the bulk of their student population. That, however, needs to change as it is recognized that there are a great many people who would benefit from part-time higher education later in life. There will surely be a major expansion in part-time higher education, in parallel with a similar expansion in tertiary and

FE colleges. But little would be gained by merging colleges and universities to form poly-versities, and a lot would be put at risk – not least the distinctive needs of younger adults, the sixteen- to nineteen year olds.

So below university and polytechnics – which incidentally should become identical in status – we need a system of tertiary colleges. Because everyone needs access to the creative arts and to technology, to the humanities and to science, to modern languages and vocational skills. Because only the tertiary college can break down the harmful and irrelevant barrier between the theoretical and the applicable. But, above all, because only the tertiary college can enable everyone to pursue their own individual excellence while learning to respect and work with all categories of other people. We need all these things. Tertiary colleges are capable of delivering them. We must make sure they do. And then we can feel confident that we shall assure our future through them.

Notes

1   NAHT, *Action Plan, A Policy 14–18* (Michael Pipes, doubtless haemorrhaging profusely, was a co-author) available from NAHT, Holly House, 6 Paddockhall Road, Haywards Heath, West Sussex RH16 1RG. SHA, *Future Imperative: A View of 16–18 and Beyond*, available from SHA, Chancery House, 107 St Pauls Road, Islington, London N1 2NB.

2.   *Towards Better Management of Secondary Education, A Report by the Audit Commission,* London, May 1986.

3.   But see Chapter 11, pp. 179, 180 for a comment on the implications of government proposals to allow schools to opt out of LEA control.

4.   See also Chapter 7 p. 82.

Bibliography

Tertiary colleges

Cotterell and Heley (eds), *Tertiary: A Radical Approach to Post-Compulsory Education*, Stanley Thorne, 1980.
Janes, Kershaw, Austin and Miles (eds), *Going Tertiary*, Tertiary Colleges Association, 1985.

Sixth-form colleges

MacFarlane, *Sixth-Form Colleges*, Heinemann, 1978.
Watkins, *The Sixth-Form College in Practice*, Edward Arnold, 1982.

Post-16 provision in general

Audit Commission, *Obtaining Better Value from Further Education*, HMSO, 1985.
Dean *et al.*, *The Sixth Form and its Alternatives,* NFER, 1979.
HMI, *NAFE in Practice. An HMI Survey*, HMSO, 1987.
Holt, *The Tertiary Sector*, Hodder & Stoughton, 1980.
King, *School and College*, Routledge & Kegan Paul, 1976.
Naylor, *Crisis in the Sixth Form*, Centre for Policy Studies (8 Wilfred Street, London SW1E 6PL), 1981.

Compendium of Sixth Form and Tertiary Colleges
  D Lavelle MA
  Winstanley College
  Billinge
  Wigan
  WN5 7XF

  £5.00 post free.

Schools

Audit Commission, *Towards the Better Management of Secondary Education*, HMSO, 1986.

Barker, *Rescuing the Comprehensive Experience*, Open University Press, 1986.

Halesowen College

Designing for Change at Halesowen, Broadsheet 14, Department of Education and Science, Architects and Buildings Group, 1983 (available free from Room 7/36, DES, Elizabeth House, York Road, London SE1 7PH).

Halesowen College internal publications are available from Halesowen College (Publications), Whittingham Road, Halesowen, West Midlands B63 3NA (please send a stamped addressed envelope for a list).

Index